PLANNING A SECURE RETIREMENT

MICHAEL JON BYERS &
MARK GROOM

This document discusses general concepts for retirement planning, and is not intended to provide tax or legal advice. Individuals are urged to consult with their tax and legal professionals regarding these issues. This handbook should ensure that clients understand a) that annuities and some of their features have costs associated with them; b) that income received from annuities is taxable; and c) that annuities used to fund IRAs do not afford any additional measure of tax deferral for the IRA owner.

Printed in the United States of America

First Printing, 2014

Gradient Positioning Systems, LLC
4105 Lexington Avenue North, Suite 110
Arden Hills, MN 55126 (877) 901-0894

ACKNOWLEDGMENTS

Over the last eighteen years I have had the wonderful pleasure of working with my best friend, Mark Groom. Mark, thank you for showing me what true friendship is.

I want to thank my wonderful kids for giving me my best reasons for doing the hard work each day. Kimberlee, Ethan, Caden and Seth, you amaze me each day. I am truly a blessed daddy to have such great kids. I have been lucky to see you grow and find your way in life. Parenting is the kind of job for which there is no practice but the blessings are unending.

Thank you, Dad, for showing me what service to this country means. Thank you for giving me the honor of being the son of an Army Dad, and for the years of travel all over the world. I would like to thank my Mom for all the life lessons she helped me through, some were harder than others.

In the process of writing this book, I have more clearly realized how blessed I am to have spent every day working with such great clients. To all of the clients we have helped over the years, and those we have yet to help, thank you for trusting us with your family, talents and retirement dreams.

Michael Jon Byers

I would first like to thank my wife of 30 years, Penny, for her support throughout the years and our journey together. She has always been there to encourage me and to raise our daughters with the values and faith that we hold dear to our hearts.

I would also like to thank my parents, Robert and Margaret Groom. They taught me the value of hard work and the value of your word. My father is a retired lieutenant colonel who flew fighter jets full-time while also running a dairy farm for 21 years. Now that's hard work!

My grandfather, Carl Rusten, who lived a long and fulfilled life for 99 years, passed down to us the saying, "measure twice and cut once." I think about that often when I'm planning a client's retirement to be sure it's right!

Mark Groom

Finally, we both would like to thank Maria Richburg, Nick Stovall, Mike Binger, Nate Lucius, Ben Mercado, Kathy Kyle and Gradient Positioning Systems, LLC, for their contributions to this project.

TABLE OF CONTENTS

INTRODUCTION

Margaret, 58, came to see us after her mother passed away. A couple of her friends, who were also our clients, recommended that we could help her with all of the paperwork, filing, and organization that would be necessary to settle her mother's estate. Margaret's mother, Annie, was a farmer's wife. She and her husband had operated a successful farm for many years, and, after his death, Annie had planned diligently to protect that legacy. Unfortunately, Annie became too ill to enjoy her retirement. Margaret, a nurse, reduced her hours to part time so that she could care for her mother and help at the farm. When her family needed her, Margaret was there. Although she had been a dedicated saver (following her parents' good example), Margaret wasn't thinking of her own savings or her retirement. She was thinking of family. And when she was forced to consider the finances, we were happy she came to us.

Don't worry: we'll return to Margaret's story soon. But first, let us introduce ourselves. We are Michael Jon Byers and Mark Groom, the financial advisors at Alliance Financial Services, including LoneStar Registered Investment Services, with our main office in Lubbock, Texas. We also have offices in Dallas, Texas and Albuquerque New Mexico. We've been advising clients since 1997 and helping them at every stage of their financial lives, and one thing we've noticed is that our clients enjoy a happier, more relaxed and fulfilling retirement if they just do three things:

- **Understand the various building blocks of their financial future**
- **Get involved with their financial planning early**
- **Stay involved**

There's good news too! We know that your financial future seems (and is) complicated. It can seem easier to simply avoid it until you have no choice but to have deal with it. But learn from the lesson of our friend Margaret: her mother's dedicated financial involvement and planning would give Margaret one of the best surprises of her life. And because of the sad loss Margaret suffered, which brought her to our door much earlier than she might have come otherwise, she now knows not only what her future financial picture looks like, but also how to shape it into any kind of future she wants. Doesn't that sound better than staying in the dark with your financial anxieties?

As for understanding the building blocks of your financial future, that's where this book comes in. We've compiled all of the basics and organized them by life stage. In the following chapters, you'll learn what you need to understand and what you need to be doing at each stage in order to create the stress-free financial future you want. Retirement timelines are different for everyone, so here are the basic guidelines:

Part One: Start Early and Finish Strong. These are considerations for your early working years, anywhere from your first day of work until you start to see retirement somewhere in your distant future, say 15 or so years away. In this stage, you're laying a solid foundation so that when it comes time to sketch out your retirement picture, you have every option available to you.

Part Two: Plan Your Retirement Dreams. This is where we start drawing the picture of what your retirement will look like. Ideally, we start this process 15 or so years before you actually retire. That gives us the leeway to make any adjustments to accommodate your desired future. Your life savings aren't the end goal: it's what those savings can DO for you that counts.

Part Three: Focus on the Finish Line. Five years prior to retirement, we start moving all of the materials into place and your actual retirement dream starts to take real shape. All of the planning we've put into your earlier years will start to bear fruit in your final working years. Unfortunately, many people don't come visit with us until this stage. If you change one thing about how you handle your financial future, let it be that one. Come see us early. If you're reading this, and you're already in this stage, find a trusted financial advisor now. Many people we meet have a great deal more assets and potential than they even know—assets that, arranged properly, could be multiplying even faster than you might imagine.

Part Four: Live Your Retirement Dream. Congratulations! This is where all your work pays off. In this stage, you get to enjoy all of the work we've done. But there are still important things to consider, as you enjoy the rewards of your work. We'll talk about how to create a plan that you can stick to, one that will ensure you have everything you need for as long as you need it, as well as a legacy to pass on.

CHOOSING YOUR FINANCIAL ADVISOR

The tricky thing about planning your financial future is that decisions you make in your thirties affect your financial picture decades later. Retirement planning is like building a bridge. Each tower and cable depends on the next to support the whole. That takes a foresight and thorough understanding of each element of your financial picture and all of the tools and vehicles that can take your finances exactly where to go. That takes more than a financial advisor. It takes a team.

YOU are the most important part of your financial team. Every bit of your retirement planning should be about ensuring that you can have the life you want when you're ready to retire, and you can provide exactly the sort of legacy you desire. So, don't just choose the financial advisor whose office is closest. Choose the one who suits YOU the best. Here's what we suggest:

Get referrals. Your friends, the people you trust, and most importantly, people who are living a retirement you admire, these are the people you ask for referrals.

Make a list, make appointments and make notes of questions you want answers to. Rather than just react to your possible advisors in the moment, know what you want. Make some notes ahead of time about what you'd like in an advisor. In your ideal meeting with your ideal advisor, what would he or she say and do? What sort of knowledge does he or she need? What is his or her philosophy?

Meet with your candidates and pay attention to how they react. Choosing your financial advisor is a highly personal process, but there are a few things that we'd encourage you to insist upon. You want an advisor who knows his/her business inside and out: every option, every tool. You want an advisor that works with a team of other financial professionals like CPA's and estate attorneys. But, most importantly, they should be asking questions about YOU. Beware of the advisor who has a lot to say about himself or herself - and asks nothing about what you want. Your advisor's job is to find out what kind of future YOU dream of, and then plan a strategy that will get you there. If you're not the focus of the meeting, it's time to meet with another advisor.

How do I decide now what my retirement dreams are? If you're starting early, retirement is a long way off. How are you supposed to know exactly what you want it to look like? Don't worry. You don't have to have an exact picture. You might already know the broad strokes. You love to travel. You're planning a large family and lots of grandkids, so there will be college and vacations. You've always wanted to have a cabin in the mountains. But even if you don't know the precise details, you know one thing for sure: when it comes time to retire, you want enough income and savings to ensure that you have as many options as possible. That means creating a plan that draws on the strength of *diversity* and *planning*.

As we said before, creating a diverse plan with strategic forethought requires a financial team. The sooner you find the right advisor for your team, the better. No doubt you've heard stories, or experienced personally, the disappointment of the 2001 recession and 2008 market corrections. Many people experienced losses that were devastating to their retirement plans.

> **As financial advisors, our goal is to ensure that our clients' personal economic situations are insulated from the greater economic situations.**

We do that by helping our clients focus their financial planning with five specific target areas. When you retire, we want to be sure that you're financially strong in five key areas:

Plenty of income. We make sure your finances are structured so that you always have enough to pay your bills, enjoy life and do the things you like to do. This could mean creating income through a personal pension or annuity. It may come partly from Social Security, and it may come from a private or government pension.

Guaranteed income. In the old days, we called this mailbox money. Today it's more like direct deposit money. This needs to be a large percentage of your income. It's money you know will show up in your account every month. Money that you know is going to be there and is not dependent on the market or determined by interest rates. This is what is called KNOW SO money.

Safe money. This money might be a principle that is creating more money (also called managed money or "Yellow Money," which we explain in Chapter 6). This money isn't what you're using right now for income, but it's safe and ready for future use.

Medical care. Healthcare is an evolving issue, but it's also one that can decimate your financial well-being if not planned for. Whether you will qualify for Medicaid, or use Medicare part A and B, with a Medicare supplement, or you'll be using a plan that's part of your retirement, we'll make sure healthcare is a planned for expense. Equally as important as preventative visits and wellness care, long term care is another expense that we will help you plan for and insure against, so that you don't lose your hard-earned nest-egg to long-term illness costs.

Final plan. Even the best planning can be undermined if attention isn't paid to settling the estate after you pass. We help our clients make a plan for when they're no longer going to be here, to protect their legacy and to make sure that family members experience the least possible effect of taxes, probate, and legal proceedings.

Uh-oh account. This might be Uh-oh, we need a new AC unit or Uh-oh, it's time to take the grandkids to Disney World! Either way, we always help our clients establish an emergency fund that sees them through unexpected expenses without getting off-plan.

The peace of mind that comes with working with someone you can trust who knows what options are available and which ones may be appropriate for you is invaluable. Choose a professional financial professional to work with who understands your needs and can connect you to the resources you need.

You will want to work with a professional who has experience in:

- IRA/401(k)/403(b)/TSP rollovers
- Federal and/or private sector retirement options
- Asset protection
- Income planning
- Wealth management
- Long-term care solutions
- Insurance
- Estate planning
- Wealth transfer strategies

The information you've read in the introduction to this book may have already changed your view on retirement. The information in the ensuing chapters can change your approach to life in retirement by giving you confidence, knowledge, and most importantly, *control* over your retirement. We hope with this information, and an advisor you trust, you're maybe even starting to get excited. With the right planning, retirement really can be one of the most rewarding times of your life.

" I BELIEVE THE POWER TO MAKE
MONEY IS A GIFT FROM GOD –
JUST AS THE INSTINCTS FOR ART,
MUSIC, LITERATURE, THE DOCTOR'S
TALENT, THE NURSE'S, YOURS – TO
BE DEVELOPED AND USED TO THE
BEST OF OUR ABILITY FOR THE
GOOD OF MANKIND. HAVING
BEEN ENDOWED WITH THE GIFT I
POSSESS, I BELIEVE IT IS MY DUTY
TO MAKE MONEY AND STILL MORE
MONEY; AND TO USE THE MONEY
I MAKE FOR THE GOOD OF MY
FELLOW MAN ACCORDING TO THE
DICTATES OF MY CONSCIENCE.

- John D. Rockefeller, Sr. "

PART ONE:
START EARLY AND FINISH STRONG

Back to Margaret. She learned a crucial financial skill from her parents: those who start early have a much better chance of finishing strong. As children of the Great Depression, Margaret's Mother and her Father were frugal, saved every chance they got, and they were quiet about having any savings at all. Margaret saved, too, just as she was taught. When her mother died, Margaret had amassed a savings of nearly $200,000, plus the 401K from her nursing job. She thought she was doing ok, but she imagined she'd only ever be able to have a meager retirement, living mostly on Social Security in a family cabin. Because her parents were so quiet about their savings, Margaret had no idea what to expect when she came to see us...

Maybe you're just starting out at your first job, and you want to start your savings strong. Or perhaps you're in your thirties or forties and turning your attention to retirement planning for the first time. Either way, we're excited you're here. Let's get started.

1

ORGANIZING YOUR ASSETS

" SOMETIMES YOUR BEST
INVESTMENTS ARE THE ONES YOU
DON'T MAKE. "

- Donald Trump

Will our Social Security benefit, savings and other retirement assets be enough? That was the question asked by the two people in our office, a couple, both retired. Richard, the husband, was 70, and his wife, Karen, was 58. The two had more than a million dollars between their savings and retirement, and no debt when they came to see us. Richard and Karen were very worried if they had enough for a comfortable retirement, and for very good reason. You see, before they *had come to see us Richard and Karen had watched their retirement accounts dwindle from $4.8 million to $1.1 million. They had saved well, but they needed a diversified plan that would help insulate their remaining retirement funds from the greater economy. Richard and Karen also needed a plan to help them create income they could count on for the rest of their lives. We helped them do that.*

Richard and Karen had a best case scenario, even after losing so much money, so it wasn't hard to help them organize their assets into a safer and more diversified plan. It was easy to make an income plan to last a lifetime by making some changes to how their savings and investments were allocated. But like most of the clients we visit with who have saved faithfully, they aren't sure how their finances will all come together to last their entire lifetimes. This is a key need in retirement making sure you have enough income to last your lifetime.

You spend your entire working life hoping what you put into your retirement accounts will help you live comfortably once you clock out of the workforce for good. The key word in that sentiment and the word that can make retirement feel like a looming problem instead of a rewarding life stage, is *hope*. You hope you'll have enough money.

Leaving your retirement up to chance is unadvisable by nearly any standard, yet millions of people find themselves hoping instead of planning for a happy ending.

With information, tools and professional guidance, creating a successful retirement plan can put you in control of your financial picture and having a successful retirement.

While you may have built up a 401(k), a 403(b), an IRA, a TSP and Social Security benefits, do you know what your financial picture really looks like?

Structuring assets to create an income-generating retirement requires a different approach than earning income via the workforce. Saving money for retirement, which is what you have spent your life doing, and *planning* your retirement are two different things. Both are important. Earning and saving money is different than creating a financial strategy that accounts for your income needs in retirement. Add the complexities of taxes, required minimum distributions (RMDs) from IRAs and legacy planning, and you can begin to see why happy endings require more than hope. They need a focused and well-executed plan.

Now that you know there's more to saving and planning for retirement than filing for your Social Security benefit and drawing income from your 401(k), 403(b), IRA or TSP, you can begin to **create a strategy for your retirement** that can have a significant impact on your financial landscape after you stop drawing a paycheck. Understanding how to manage your assets entails risk management, risk diversification, tax planning and income planning preparation throughout your life stages. These strategies can help you leverage more from each one of the hard-earned dollars you set aside for your retirement.

Some people file for Social Security on day one of their retirement. Others rely on supplemental income from an IRA or another retirement account. Working with a financial professional can help you determine your best course of action.

NEW IDEAS FOR RETIREMENT

Advice about what to do with money has been around as long as money has existed. Hindsight allows us to see which advice was good and which advice didn't cut the mustard. Some sources of advice have been around for a very long time. While there are some basic investment concepts that have stood the test of time, most strategies that work adapt to changing conditions in the market, in the economy and the world, as well as changes in your personal circumstances.

The reality is that investment strategies and savings plans that worked in the past have encountered challenging new circumstances that have turned them on their heads. The recessions in 2000 and 2008 both highlighted how old investment ideas were not only ineffective but incredibly destructive to the retirement plans of millions of Americans. The dawn of an entirely restructured health care system brings with it new options and challenges that will undoubtedly change the way insurance companies provide investment products and services.

Perhaps the most important lessons investors learned from the Great Recession of 2008 is that not understanding where your money is invested (and the potential risks of those investments) can work against you, your plans for retirement and your legacy. Saving and investing money isn't enough to truly get the most out of it. You must have a planful approach to managing your assets.

Essentially, managing your money and your investments is an ongoing process that requires customization and adaptation to a changing world. And make no mistake; the world is always changing. What worked for your parents or even your parents' parents was probably good advice back then. People in retirement or approaching retirement today need new ideas and professional guidance.

HOPE SO VS. KNOW SO MONEY

Let's take a look at some of the basic truths about money as it relates to saving for retirement.

There are essentially two kinds of money: *Hope So* and *Know So.*

Everyone can divide their money into these two categories. Some have more of one kind than the other. The goal isn't to eliminate one kind of money but to balance them as you approach retirement.

Hope So Money is money that is at risk. It fluctuates with the market. It has no minimum guarantee. It is subject to investor activity, stock prices, market trends, buying trends, etc. You get the picture. This money is exposed to more risk but also has the potential for more reward. Because the market is subject to change, you can't really be sure what the value of your investments will be worth in the future. You can't really *rely* on it at all. For this reason, we refer to it as Hope So Money. This doesn't mean you shouldn't have some money invested in the market, but it would be dangerous to assume you can know what it will be worth in the future.

Hope So Money is an important element of a retirement plan, especially in the early stages of planning when you can trade volatility for potential returns, and when a longer investment timeframe is available to you. In the long run, time can smooth out the ups and downs of money exposed to the market. Working with a professional and leveraging a long-term investment strategy has the potential to create rewarding returns from Hope So Money.

Know So Money, on the other hand, is safer when compared to Hope So Money. Know So Money is made up of dependable, low-risk or no-risk money, and investments that you can count on. Social Security is one of the most common forms of Know So Money. Income you draw or will draw from Social Security is guaranteed. You have paid into Social Security your entire career, and you can rely on that money during your retirement. Unlike the market, rates of growth for Know So Money are dependent on 10-year treasury rates. The 10-year treasury, or TNX, is commonly considered to represent a very secure and safe place for your money, hence Know So Money. The 10-year treasury drives key rates for things such as mortgage rates or CD rates. Know So

Money may not be as exciting as Hope So Money, but it is safer. You can safely be fairly sure you will have it in the future.

Knowing the difference between Hope So and Know So Money is an important step towards a successful retirement plan. People who are 55 or older and who are looking ahead to retirement should be relying on more Know So Money than Hope So Money.

Ideally, the rates of return on Hope So and Know So Money would have an overlapping area that provided an acceptable rate of risk for both types of money. In the early 1990s, interest rates were high and market volatility was low. At that time, you could invest in either Hope So or Know So Money options because the rates of return were similar from both Know So and Hope So investments, and you were likely to be fairly successful with a wide range of investment options. At that time, you could expose yourself to an acceptable amount of risk or an acceptable fixed rate. Basically, it was difficult to make a mistake during that time period. Today, you don't have those options. Market volatility is at all-time highs while interest rates are at all-time lows. They are so far apart from each other that it is hard to know what to do with your money.

> **Yesterday's investment rules may not work today. Not only could they hamper achieving your goals, they may actually harm your financial situation.**

We are currently in a period when the rates for Know So Money options are at historic lows, and the volatility of Hope So Money is higher than ever. There is no overlapping acceptable rate, making both options less than ideal. *Because of this uncertain financial landscape, wise investment strategies are more important now than ever.*

This unique situation requires fresh ideas and investment tools that haven't been relied on in the past. Investing the way your parents did will not pay off. The majority of investment ideas used by financial professionals in the 1990s aren't applicable to today's markets. That kind of investing will likely get you in trouble and compromise your retirement. Today, you need a better PLAN.

HOW MUCH RISK ARE *YOU* EXPOSED TO?

Many investors don't know how much risk they are exposed to. It is helpful to organize your assets so you can have a clear understanding of how much of your money is at risk and how much is in safer holdings. This process starts with listing all your assets.

Let's take a look at the two kinds of money:

Hope So Money is, as the name indicates, money that you *hope* will be there when you need it. Hope So Money represents what you would like to get out of your investments. Examples of Hope So Money include:

- Stock market funds, including index funds
- Mutual funds
- Variable annuities
- REITS

Know So Money is money that you know you can count on. It is safer money that isn't exposed to the level of volatility as the asset types noted above. You can more confidently count on having this money when you need it. Examples of Know So Money are:

- Government backed bonds
- Savings and checking accounts
- Fixed income annuities
- CDs
- Treasuries or bonds
- Fixed index annuities

- Money market accounts

> *» Ben had a modest brokerage account that he added to when he could. When he changed jobs a couple years ago, at age 58, Ben transferred his 401(k) assets into an IRA. Just a few years from retirement, he is now beginning to realize that nearly every dollar he has saved for retirement is subject to market risk.*
>
> *Intuitively, he knows that the time has come to shift some assets to an alternative that is safer, but how much is the right amount? He knows he cannot afford to lose 30 percent or 40 percent of his 401(k) or IRA like he did in the market downturn of 2008.*

HOW MUCH RISK?

Determining the amount of risk that is right for you is dependent on a number of variables. You need to feel comfortable with where and how you are investing your money, and your financial professional is obligated to help you make decisions that put your money in places that fit your risk criteria.

Your retirement needs to first accommodate your day-to-day income needs. How much money do you need to maintain your lifestyle? When do you need it?

Managing your risk by having a balance of Hope So Money vs. Know So Money is a good start that will put you ahead of the curve. But how much Know So Money is enough to secure your income needs during retirement, and how much Hope So Money is enough to allow you to continue to benefit from an improving market?

In short, how do you begin to know how much risk you should be exposed to?

While there is no single approach to investment risk determination advice that is universally applicable to everyone, there are some helpful guidelines. One of the oldest is called *The Rule of 100*.

The average investor needs to accumulate assets or investments and savings to create a retirement plan that provides income during retirement and also allows for legacy planning. To accomplish this, they need to balance the amount of risk to which they are exposed. Risk is required because, while Know So Money is safer, more reliable and more dependable, it doesn't grow very fast, if at all. Today's historically low interest rates barely break even with current inflation. Hope So Money, while less dependable, has more potential for growth. Hope So Money can eventually become Know So Money once you move it to an investment with lower risk. Everyone's risk diversification will be different depending on their goals, age and their existing assets.

So how do you decide how much risk your assets should be exposed to? Where do you begin? Luckily, there's a guideline you can use to start making decisions about risk management. It's called the Rule of 100.

THE RULE OF 100

The Rule of 100 is a general rule that helps shape asset diversification* for the average investor. The rule states that the number 100 minus an investor's age equals the amount of assets they should have exposed to risk.

The Rule of 100: 100 - (your age) = the percentage of your assets that should be exposed to risk (Hope So Money)

53   47

should be about 50/50 — safe/risk

Asset Diversification disclosure — Diversification and asset allocation does not assure of guarantee better performance and cannot eliminate the risk of investment loss. Before investing, you should carefully read the applicable volatility disclosure for each of the underlying funds, which can be found in the current prospectus.

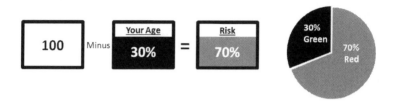

For example, if you are a 30-year-old investor, the Rule of 100 would indicate that you should be focusing on investing primarily in the market and taking on a substantial amount of risk in your portfolio. The Rule of 100 suggests that 70 percent of your investments should be exposed to risk.

$$100 - (30 \text{ years of age}) = 70 \text{ percent}$$

Now, not every 30-year-old should have exactly 70 percent of their assets in mutual funds and stocks. The Rule of 100 is based on your chronological age, not your "financial age," which could vary based on your investment experience, your aversion or acceptance of risk and other factors. While this rule isn't an ironclad solution to anyone's finances, it's a pretty good place to start. Once you've taken the time to look at your assets with a professional to determine your risk exposure, you can use the Rule of 100 to make changes that put you in a more stable investment position — one that reflects your comfort level.

Perhaps when you were age 30 and starting your career, like in the example above, it made sense to have 70 percent of your money in the market: you had time on your side. You had plenty of time to save more money, work more and recover from a downturn in the market. Retirement was ages away, and your earning power was increasing. And indeed, younger investors should take on more risk for exactly those reasons. The potential reward of long-term involvement in the market outweighs the risk of investing when you are young.

Risk tolerance generally reduces as you get older, however. If you are 40 years old and lose 30 percent of your portfolio in a market downturn this year, you have 20 or 30 years to recover it. If you are 68 years old, you have five to 10 years (or less) to make the same recovery. That new circumstance changes your whole retirement perspective. At age 68, it's likely that you simply aren't as interested in suffering through a tough stock market. There is less time to recover from downturns, and the stakes are higher. The money you have saved is money you will soon need to provide you with income, or is money that you already need to meet your income demands.

Much of the flexibility that comes with investing earlier in life is related to *compounding*. Compounded earnings can be incredibly powerful over time. The longer your money has time to compound, the greater your wealth will be. This is what most people talk about when they refer to putting their money to work. This is also why the Rule of 100 favors risk for the young. If you start investing when you are young, you can invest smaller amounts of money in a more aggressive fashion because you have the potential to make a profit in a rising market and you can harness the power of compounding earnings. When you are 40, 50 or 60 years old, that potential becomes less and less and you are forced to have more money at lower amounts of risk to realize the same returns. **It basically becomes more expensive to prudently invest the older you get.**

You risk not having a recovery period the older you get, so should have less of your assets at risk in volatile investments. You should shift with the Rule of 100 to protect your assets and ensure that they will provide you with the income you need in retirement. Let's look at another example that illustrates how the Rule of 100 becomes more critical as you age. An 80-year-old investor who is retired and is relying on retirement assets for income, for example, needs to depend on a solid amount of Know So Money. The Rule of 100 says an 80-year-old investor should have a maximum of 20 percent of his or her assets at risk. Depending on the investor's financial position, even less risk exposure may be required. You are the only person who can make this kind of determination, but the Rule of 100 can help. Everyone has their own level of comfort. Your Rule of 100 results will be based on your values and attitudes as well as your comfort with risk.

The Rule of 100 can apply to overarching financial management and to specific investment products that you own as well. Take the 401(k) for example. Many people have them, but not many people understand how their money is allocated within their 401(k). An employer may have someone who comes in once a year and explains the models and options that employees can choose from, but that's as much guidance as most 401(k) holders get. Many 401(k) options include target date funds that change their risk exposure over time, essentially following a form of the Rule of 100. Selecting one of these options can often be a good move for employees because they shift your risk as you age, securing more Know So Money when you need it.

A financial professional can look at your investments and savings with you and discuss alternatives to optimize your balance between Know So and Hope So Money.

CHAPTER 1 RECAP //

- There is money you hope you'll have in the future, and there's money you know you'll have in the future. Make sure you know how much you need when you retire.
- Organizing your assets starts with making a list. You can then understand how each asset is balanced for risk.
- Your exposure to risk is ultimately determined by you.

- Use the Rule of 100 as a general guiding principle when determining how much risk your retirement investments should be exposed to (100 - [your age] = [percentage of your investments that can comfortably exposed to risk])

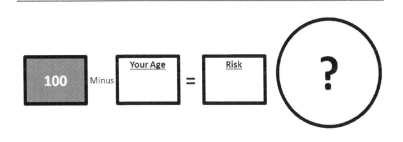

2

NEW IDEAS FOR INVESTING

In Chapter 1, we discussed how today's investment options require advice that is relevant to today. Traditional, outdated investment strategies are not only ineffective, they can be harmful to the average investor. One of the most traditional ways of thinking about investing is the risk versus reward trade-off. It goes something like this.

Investment options that are considered safer carry less risk, but also offer the potential for less return. Riskier investment options carry the burden of volatility and a greater potential for loss, but they also offer a greater potential for large rewards. Most professionals move their clients back and forth along this range, shifting between investments that are safer and investments that are structured for growth. Essentially, the old rules of investing dictate that you can either choose relative safety *or* return, but you can't have both.

Updated investment strategies work with the flexibility of liquidity to remake the rules. Here is how:

There are three dimensions that are inherent in any investment: *Liquidity, Safety,* and *Return.* You can maximize any two of these dimensions at the expense of the third. If you choose Safety and Liquidity, this is like keeping your assets in a checking account or savings account. This option delivers a lot of Safety and Liquidity, but at the expense of any Return. On the other hand, if you choose Liquidity and Return, meaning you have the potential for great return and can still reclaim your money whenever you choose, you will likely be exposed to a very high level of risk.

Understanding Liquidity can help you break the old Risk versus Safety trade-off. By identifying assets from which you don't require Liquidity, you can place yourself in a position to potentially profit from relatively safe investments that provide a higher than average rate of return.

Choosing Safety and Return over Liquidity can have significant impacts on the accumulation of your assets. In Ted's case, the paradigm shift from earning and saving to leveraging assets was a costly one.

> » *Ted is a corn and soybean farmer with 1,200 acres of land he also raises some cattle. He routinely retains somewhere between $40,000 and $80,000 in his checking and savings accounts. If a major piece of equipment fails and needs repair or replacement, Ted will need the money available to pay for the equipment and carry on with farming. If the price of feed for his cattle goes up one year, he will need to compensate for the increased overhead to his farming operation. He isn't a particularly wealthy farmer, but he has little choice but to keep a portion of money on hand in case something comes up*

and he must access it quickly. Most of his capital is held in livestock in the pasture or crops in the ground tied up for six to eight months of the year. When a major financial need arises, Ted can't just harvest 10 acres of soybeans and use them for payment. He needs to depend heavily on Liquidity in order to be a successful farmer.

Old habits die hard, however, and when Ted finally hangs up his overalls and quits farming, he keeps his bank accounts flush with cash, just like in the old days. After selling the farm and the equipment, Ted keeps a huge portion of the profits in Liquid investments because that's what he is familiar with. Unfortunately for Ted, with his pile of money sitting in his checking account, he isn't even keeping pace with inflation. After all his hard work as a farmer, his money is losing value every day because he didn't shift to a paradigm of leveraging his assets to generate income and accumulate value.

Almost anything would be a better option for Ted than clinging to Liquidity. He could have done something better to get more return from his money with keeping the safety he needs and feels comfortable with, and at the very least would not have lost out to inflation.

As you can see, choosing Liquidity only can be a costly option. The sooner you want your money back, the less you can leverage it for Safety or Return. If you have the option of putting your money in a long-term investment, you will be sacrificing Liquidity, but potentially keeping Safety and increasing Returns. Re-thinking your approach to money in this way can make a world of difference and can provide you with a structured way to generate income while allowing the value of your asset to grow over time.

The question is, how much Liquidity do you *really* need?

Think about it. If you haven't sat down and created an income plan for your retirement, your perceived need for Liquidity is a guess. You don't know how much cash you'll need to fill the income gap if you don't know the amount of your Social Security benefit of the total of your other income options. If you *have* determined your income need and have made a plan for filling your income gap, you can partition your assets based on when you will need them. With an income plan in place, ***you can use new rules to enjoy both Safety and Return from your assets.***

CHAPTER 2 RECAP //

- Understanding Liquidity can help you break the old Risk versus Safety trade-off. By identifying assets from which you don't require Liquidity, you can place yourself in a position to potentially profit from relatively safe investments that provide a higher than average rate of return.
- Choosing Safety and Return over Liquidity can have significant impacts on the accumulation of your assets. Updated investment strategies work with the flexibility of liquidity to remake the rules.

3

RETIREMENT STICKERS VERSUS VEHICLES

One of the common misconceptions we run into is how you're getting to retirement. If you ask a person how they're planning to get to retirement, they'll most often reply, "I have a 401(k)," or "I get a pension." But those aren't vehicles that go anywhere. 401(k)s, Roth IRAs, TSP and pensions are just types of accounts; they're like the stickers that go on the vehicles, showing what they're approved to do, like pass through the tax-free tollbooth or just tax deferred toll both. They don't have anything to do with how your money is invested, grows, what sort of risk you're running, and what sort of return you might expect. All of those are critical components in your financial planning strategy.

For example, in your early working years, you might want a Ferrari or *Tesla* Roadster investment vehicle: higher speed, but higher risk. As you get closer to retirement, though, you want to move most of your money into a more dependable, lower risk vehicle such as a Camry, GMC Truck or Chevrolet Impala perhaps.

> **The sort of investment vehicle you have depends on a number of factors, and you'll get the best results if you work with a trusted advisor.**

The type of retirement sticker, however, often depends on your job, as well as whether that job is in the private sector or as a public employee. We work with a number of federal employees, and so at Alliance Financial Services, we've developed expertise in managing all types of retirement accounts. In the following chapters, you'll find a basic primer on the various types of accounts, both public and private.

Raymond came to see us a few years ago. He was 44, and we were excited to meet with him so early in his career. Soon we learned that Raymond had been working as a federal employee for 15 years, and had been contributing to his Thrift Savings Plan (TSP) or Government 401(K) equivalent, all during that time. So far everything looked great. However, he hadn't learned, when setting up his TSP and contributions, that he was eligible for a maximum five percent matching contribution from the government. Because he didn't know about the match, Raymond had elected to go with the mandatory 1 percent contribution, which meant he was leaving a huge amount of money behind every year. He was leaving free money on the table every year. Take all the free money you can get. If your employer offers a match for a 401(k), 403(b), TSP or other retirement saving options, take them up on all the free money or match they give you. Everyone should love free money and get all you can.

It was sad that Raymond had missed out on some potential savings, but what a great thing that he decided to come see us so early. We were able to help him make up for a lot of that loss as well as maximize all of his future savings. It's not uncommon, though, especially among federal employees, for clients to wait until five or ten years before retirement to come see us. If Raymond had put off his visit to us until then, he'd have lost an additional 10-15 years of the government match he was entitled to, and a huge chunk of his retirement.

Learn from Raymond's story. We can't stress that enough. It's so crucial that you know all of the ins and outs of your employer's retirement program. Sometimes it can be difficult, especially with the rush and hustle of starting a new job, to know all of the right questions to ask your Human Resources representative. Just one meeting with a financial advisor, early in your career, could save you thousands of lost dollars in your retirement.

In preparation for that meeting and your own financial planning, it's helpful to know the basics of the retirement system and what your employer offers.

CHAPTER 3 RECAP //

- A 401(k), Roth IRA, TSP or pension plan isn't your investment vehicle. It's your savings plan, and acts more like the sticker that says which tollbooths (e.g. tax free or tax deferred) your money can go through.
- Knowing what investment vehicle you have is crucial, as they come with different risks and rewards.

4
SAVING DURING GOVERNMENT SERVICE

Because we have worked with a lot of Federal employees all over the country for many years, we wanted to include a chapter just for those federal employees. If you have not worked for the federal government and do not plan on getting a job with the federal government, feel free to skip this chapter and go on to the next chapter.

If you work for the federal government, a state government, a railroad, or if you are in the military, your retirement benefits may be subject to special rules. You should know how your retirement plan works, what distribution rules apply, how your survivors can benefit, how your plan may be integrated with Social Security, and what tax rules apply.

THE FEDERAL EMPLOYEES RETIREMENT SYSTEM (FERS)

Most federal employees hired on or after January 1, 1984, are automatically covered by the FERS, a three-tier retirement system encompassing benefits provided by Social Security (tier one), the Basic Benefit Plan (tier two), and the Thrift Savings Plan (tier three). They work together like the three legs of a stool,

What benefits are provided under FERS?

Social Security benefits

Unlike workers covered under the older Civil Service Retirement System (CSRS), federal workers under FERS pay Social Security taxes on their earnings. This means that if you are covered by FERS, you are also entitled to receive Social Security benefits (including Medicare) when eligible. However, the benefits you receive under FERS are designed to coordinate with the Social Security benefits you receive.

Basic Benefit FERS annuity and supplement

The heart of FERS is the Basic Benefit Plan. This plan pays retirement, survivor, and disability benefits to qualified FERS employees. Most FERS Basic Benefits are paid as monthly annuities. To be eligible for benefits, you have to meet certain length-of-service requirements and, in the case of retirement benefits, age requirements. The amount of retirement benefit you receive will depend on your average pay, high three and the age at which you retired. If you retire before becoming eligible to receive Social Security retirement benefits (age 62), you may receive a Special Retirement Supplement in addition to your basic annuity. This supplement approximates the Social Security benefit you earned while employed by the federal government.

This Social Security supplement is from FERS and ends at age 62 whether or not you choose to start Social Security at age 62.

Example: Clarissa retired at age 60 after she had worked for the federal government for 20 years. She began receiving a retirement annuity under FERS. Since she was not yet eligible to receive Social Security benefits, she also received a supplemental annuity. She continued to receive the supplemental annuity until she turned 62 and became eligible for Social Security retirement benefits.

Eligibility
Eligibility is determined by your age and number of years of creditable service. In some cases, you must have reached the Minimum Retirement Age (MRA) to receive retirement benefits. Use the following chart to figure your Minimum Retirement Age.

ELIGIBILITY INFORMATION

IF YOU WERE BORN	YOUR MRA IS
Before 1948	55
In 1948	55 and 2 months
In 1949	55 and 4 months
In 1950	55 and 6 months
In 1951	55 and 8 months
In 1952	55 and 10 months
In 1953-1964	56
In 1965	56 and 2 months
In 1966	56 and 4 months
In 1967	56 and 6 months
In 1968	56 and 8 months
In 1969	56 and 10 months
In 1970 and after	57

Immediate Retirement

An immediate retirement benefit is one that starts within 30 days from the date you stop working. If you meet one of the following sets of age and service requirements, you are entitled to an immediate retirement benefit:

ELIGIBILITY INFORMATION

AGE	YEARS OF SERVICE
62	5
60	20
MRA	30
MRA	10

If you retire at the MRA with at least 10, but less than 30 years of service, your benefit will be reduced by 5 percent a year for each year you are under 62, unless you have 20 years of service and your benefit starts when you reach age 60 or later.

Early Retirement

The early retirement benefit is available in certain involuntary separation cases and in cases of voluntary separations during a major reorganization or reduction in force. To be eligible, you must meet the following requirements:

ELIGIBILITY INFORMATION

AGE	YEARS OF SERVICE
50	20
Any Age	25

Deferred Retirement

Refers to delayed payment of benefit until criteria are met, as follows:

If you leave Federal service before you meet the age and service requirements for an immediate retirement benefit, you may be eligible for deferred retirement benefits. To be eligible, you must have completed at least 5 years of creditable civilian service. You may receive benefits when you reach one of the following ages:

ELIGIBILITY INFORMATION

AGE	YEARS OF SERVICE
62	5
MRA	30
MRA	10

If you retire at the MRA with at least 10, but less than 30 years of service, your benefit will be reduced by 5 percent a year for each year you are under 62, unless you have 20 years of service and your benefit starts when you reach age 60 or later.

COMPUTATION FOR NON-DISABILITY RETIREMENTS

FERS BASIC ANNUITY FORMULA

AGE	FORMULA
Under Age 62 at Separation for Retirement, OR Age 62 or Older With Less Than 20 Years of Service	1 percent of your high-3 average salary for each year of service
Age 62 or Older at Separation With 20 or More Years of Service	1.1 percent of your high-3 average salary for each year of service

Military Service

The federal government allows you to purchase back your military time and add it to your FERS or CSRS annuity. This is a huge benefit for those that have served our country. It almost always makes sense to buy back military time and add it to your annuity.

The sooner you buy this time back the cheaper it is but even if you buy it back just before retirement it will be worth it for you. The following example illustrates some of these options:

> » John is a federal employee age 62 and is looking at retirement this next year. Like we hear so often John was told not to buy his 5 years in the Army back and add them to his federal time. This was so not true. Let's look at the numbers. The cost to John buying back his 5 years in the Army today is $6,000. If John buys back this time, his retirement annuity will be $400 more a month for the rest of his life. So if you take the $6000 and divide it by the extra $400 a month John will be getting in retirement for the rest of his life, he will recover his $6000 in only 15 months. If John plans on living longer than fifteen months after he retires he will be getting $400 a month more than the cost of buying back that time for every month past the initial fifteen months.

Credit for Military Service

As a general rule, military service in the Armed Forces of the United States is creditable for retirement purposes if it was active service terminated under honorable conditions, and performed prior to your separation from civilian service for retirement.

Service Performed Before 1957

- Creditable without deposit

Service Performed on or after January 1, 1957

- A deposit must be paid to credit the service to establish title to an annuity or to compute your annuity

How is FERS funded?

FERS is funded by contributions from both the employee and the federal government. The following table illustrates how FERS is funded:

FERS BENEFIT	EMPLOYEE CONTRIBUTION	FEDERAL GOVERNMENT (EMPLOYER) CONTRIBUTION
Social Security (including Medicare)	7.65 percent of earnings up to maximum wage base	7.65 percent of earnings up to maximum wage base
Basic Benefit Plan	.80 percent of earnings	Varies according to formula
Thrift Savings Plan	Up to 100 percent of the basic pay earned each pay period, up to the IRS limit of $17,500 in 2013 ($17,000 in 2012)*	1 percent of basic pay plus $1 of every dollar employee contributes up to 3 percent of basic pay; 50 cents for every dollar employee contributes thereafter, up to a total of 5 percent of basic pay each pay period

Who is covered under FERS?

Most federal employees hired on or after January 1, 1984, are automatically covered by FERS.

Employees who transfer to FERS from the Civil Service Retirement System

You may also be covered by FERS if you elected to transfer to the system from the CSRS during a special transfer period in 1987. You may also be covered by FERS if you previously worked for the government under CSRS, left government service, and are now working for the federal government again. In this case, you are automatically covered if you left federal government service and returned after more than one year and you have less than five years under CSRS. Otherwise, you may have to transfer to FERS under special rules. For information on transferring to FERS, contact your agency's personnel office or the Office of Personnel Management's website at www.opm.gov.

> **Example:** Karen worked for the federal government under CSRS from 1993 to 1995. In 2013, she was re-employed by the federal government. Because she had less than five years of CSRS service and returned to federal service after being away from it for more than a year, Karen was now automatically covered by FERS.

Employees excluded from coverage

A few employees are specifically excluded from coverage under FERS. These employees include persons not covered by Social Security, employees whose appointments are limited to one year or less, and certain persons with non-federal service that is creditable under the Civil Service Retirement System.

Special groups of employees covered by FERS

A few groups of employees are paid annuities according to special rules:

GROUP	CONDITIONS	BENEFIT
Firefighters, Law Enforcement Officers and Air Traffic Controllers	Contribute an extra 0.5 percent of pay to FERS	Can receive unreduced benefit at age 50 with 20 years of service or at any age with 25 years of service. The annual annuity is 1.7 percent of high-3 average pay times years of service plus 1.0 percent of high-3 average pay times years of service exceeding 20
Military Reserve Technicians	Loses military status required to maintain position	May retire and receive an unreduced annuity if you are at least age 50 with 25 years of service
Part-Time Employees	None	In calculating annuity, average high-3 consecutive years of pay will be based on full-time rate, then reduced according to part-time schedule
Members of Congress and Congressional Employees	Contribute an extra 0.5 percent of pay to FERS	Members of Congress receive an unreduced annuity at age 50 with 20 years of service or at any age with 25 years. Congressional employees are subject to same rules as other employees. Annuities for both groups with at least 5 years of Congressional service will be 1.7 percent of high-3 average pay times years of service up to 20 plus 1 percent of high-3 average pay times any other service

The Thrift Savings Plan

Similar to a 401(k) plan, the Thrift Savings Plan (TSP) is a tax-deferred retirement savings vehicle automatically set up for employees under FERS. The government contributes 1 percent of your basic pay each pay period to the plan and matches (up to a certain limit--see table below) contributions you make to the plan. Your contributions can be pre-tax or Roth (or a combination of the two).

Example: Marcus retired from government service at age 62. Over the years, he had only contributed 3 percent of his basic pay each pay period to his TSP. The government had matched those contributions dollar for dollar and also contributed an additional 1 percent of Marcus 's basic pay to his account each pay period. By the time Marcus retired, he had accumulated over $70,000 in his thrift account. He elected to receive an annuity that paid him $575 a month for the rest of his life.

This annuity is for just Marcus's life, so his family will not get any money after Marcus dies. We do not suggest this type of annuity in most cases. Also, Marcus gave up free money during his whole federal employment time because the government would have matched 5 percent. Don't do this; take all the free money you can.

A life annuity provides guaranteed monthly payments for as long as you are alive. If you want a life annuity that pays benefits to a survivor, or joint annuitant, you have that option as well. We suggest that you look at options in the private sector. The TSP life annuity is one of the full withdrawal options that are available to you once you have left the Federal Government or the uniformed services.

> **Make sure you do not confuse the TSP annuity that you can purchase as a full withdrawal option with the annuity that is part of your retirement package.**

The TSP annuity is not the basic annuity that you will receive when you retire as either a FERS or CSRS employee, or the retired pay that you receive as a member of the uniformed services.

THE CIVIL SERVICE RETIREMENT SYSTEM (CSRS)

What is the Civil Service Retirement System (CSRS)?

Federal employees hired before January 1, 1984, were automatically covered by CSRS, which was created in 1920. CSRS covered most federal employees until the Federal Employees Retirement System (FERS) was enacted. Today, most federal workers are covered by FERS, in part because federal workers who were covered by CSRS had the chance to transfer to FERS during a 1987 transfer period. Like employees covered by FERS, CSRS employees may be eligible for retirement and disability benefits, and if they die, their survivors may be eligible for survivor annuities or lump-sum death benefits. CSRS employees are also entitled to contribute to the Thrift Savings Plan on a limited basis.

How is CSRS funded?

CSRS is funded by contributions from both the employee and the federal government. Most employees contribute 7 percent of their basic pay (members of Congress, Congressional employees, law enforcement officers, certain air traffic controllers, and firefighters may have different contribution percentages). The government agency for which they work matches those contributions. Additional funds for the program come from the General Treasury.

RETIREMENT BENEFITS UNDER CSRS

Eligibility requirements

To be eligible to receive a CSRS retirement annuity, you must have worked for the federal government as a civilian for at least five full years. In addition, you must have been employed under CSRS for at least one year out of the last two years before you retired or separated from government service, unless you are retiring on disability.

Immediate annuity

If you retire or separate from government service, you may be entitled to receive an immediate annuity by meeting certain age and length-of-service requirements. You will receive your first annuity payment on the first day of the month following the month you stopped working. For instance, if you retire on any day during September, your annuity will begin on October 1. The following table outlines age and length-of-service requirements for immediate annuities:

TYPE OF RETIREMENT	MINIMUM AGE	MINIMUM YEARS OF SERVICE
OPTIONAL	62 60 55	5 20 30
SPECIAL OPTIONAL (LAW ENFORCEMENT OFFICERS AND FIREFIGHTERS)	50	20
SPECIAL OPTIONAL (AIR TRAFFIC CONTROLLERS)	50 ANY AGE	20 25
EARLY OPTIONAL (AGENCY REDUCTION IN FORCE, REORGANIZATION, TRANSFER OF FUNCTION)	50* ANY AGE*	20 25
DISCONTINUED SERVICE (INVOLUNTARY SEPARATION)	50* ANY AGE*	20 25
DISABILITY	ANY AGE	5

Deferred annuity

If you leave federal employment and are not yet eligible for an immediate annuity, you have two choices: You can withdraw your contributions to CSRS, or you can leave the money in the system. If you've completed at least five years of civilian service and you

*Annuity reduced if under age 55 and separated involuntarily. The annuity is reduced by one-sixth of 1 percent for each full month the employee is under age 55 (2 percent per year).

leave your money in the system, you will be entitled to receive a deferred annuity at age 62.

> **Caution:** Before choosing to leave your money in the system, however, determine if the CSRS annuity you receive will affect your future Social Security benefit. If you will be entitled to a Social Security retirement benefit because you worked in a job where you paid Social Security taxes, your CSRS pension may affect how your Social Security retirement benefit is calculated. In addition, if you receive a government pension and you also receive a spousal Social Security retirement or survivor's benefit, your Social Security benefit may be reduced.

Alternative Form of Annuity

If you are retired and have a life-threatening illness or medical condition, you may be able to receive a reduced monthly benefit plus a lump-sum payment of your un-refunded contributions to the retirement fund in lieu of a regular retirement annuity. For more information, check with the Office of Personnel Management (OPM).

> **Caution:** You can't be retired under disability rules or have a former spouse entitled to court-ordered benefits, and you must have your spouse's consent to elect an Alternative Form of Annuity.

Forms of retirement annuities

At the time you retire, you can elect to receive your annuity in one of three ways:

1. Payment of an annuity to you for life
2. Payment of an annuity to you for life, with a survivor annuity payable to your spouse for life after you die

3. Payment of an annuity to you for life, with an insurable interest annuity paid to your beneficiary after you die

Benefit amount

Your retirement annuity is computed based on your length of creditable service and your high-3 average pay. The annuity is computed by adding:

- 1.5 percent of your high-3 average pay
- multiplied by service up to 5 years
- plus 1.75 percent of your high-3 average pay
- multiplied by years of service over 5 and up to 10
- plus 2 percent of your high-3 average pay
- multiplied by years of service over 10

Example: Bonita's high-3 average pay is calculated to be $20,000. She worked for the government for 30 years, so her annuity is calculated as follows:

1.5 percent x $20,000 x 5 years	=	$ 1,500
1.75 percent x $20,000 x 5 years	=	$ 1,750
2 percent x $20,000 x 20 years	=	$ 8,000
	=	$11,250

SURVIVOR BENEFITS UNDER CSRS

Eligibility requirements

If you die while you are actively employed by the federal government after 18 months of civilian service, your spouse will be entitled to an annuity if you were married for at least 9 months. However, if your death was accidental or if there is a child of the marriage, the 9-month rule does not apply.

If you die while actively employed by the federal government but before you have worked 18 months, or you have no widow, former spouse, or children who are eligible for a survivor annuity, your named beneficiary will receive a lump-sum payment equal to your contribution to CSRS, plus any accrued interest. (No interest is payable if you paid into CSRS for less than one year.)

Spouse's benefit

If you die before retirement from service: Your spouse will be entitled to receive 55 percent of the basic annuity you had earned at the time of your death or, if it will result in a higher benefit, 55 percent of the guaranteed minimum benefit.

If you die after retirement from service: If you are married, your retirement annuity will automatically be reduced to include a survivor annuity for your spouse unless you and your spouse waive this in writing. Your annuity will be reduced by 2.5 percent of the first $3,600, plus 10 percent of the annuity over $3,600. Your spouse will usually receive this annuity until he or she dies or remarries (prior to age 55). You can elect to provide your spouse either a full survivor annuity or, if your spouse consents, a reduced survivor annuity. Your spouse will receive 55 percent of the annuity you were receiving.

> **Example:** Evelyn retired from government service and began receiving an immediate annuity but reduced to provide a survivor annuity for her husband. Her annuity of $1,926 was reduced to $1,878, which she received monthly for five years. When she died, her husband began receiving a monthly annuity equal to 55 percent of Evelyn's unreduced annuity, or $1,059.

Former spouse's benefit

If you were divorced after May 6, 1985, your former spouse may receive all or part of your survivor annuity by court order. Or, if your current spouse agrees to it, you can elect a survivor annuity for your former spouse when you retire.

Child's benefit

If you die while employed by the federal government, your unmarried children under 18 (22, if in school full-time) will receive an annuity. A child over age 18 who is disabled will also receive an annuity if the child's disability began before age 18 and if the child is dependent on you for support.

An insurable interest benefit

You can also elect to reduce your retirement annuity to provide a survivor annuity to a person who has an insurable interest in you. This might be someone who depends on your income, such as a dependent parent. You might also elect to provide an insurable interest annuity to your current spouse if he or she is ineligible to receive an annuity because your former spouse has a right to a court-ordered survivor annuity. To provide an insurable interest annuity, your annuity would be reduced between 10 percent and 40 percent, depending on the difference in age between you and the beneficiary named.

> **Caution:** You must be in reasonably good health and not retiring as a result of disability to provide an insurable interest survivor annuity. This annuity can be elected in addition to a regular survivor annuity.

Questions & Answers

Can you receive both a retirement annuity under CSRS and a Social Security survivor's benefit based on your spouse's earnings?

Yes. If your spouse paid Social Security taxes and is entitled to Social Security benefits, you may be entitled to a Social Security survivor's benefit. However, because you also receive a retirement annuity under CSRS, the amount of Social Security survivor's benefit you receive may be reduced. This reduction, known as the government pension offset, will reduce your Social Security benefits by two-thirds of the amount of your government pension. So, for instance, if you receive $600 a month from your CSRS annuity and would normally be entitled to a $500 benefit from Social Security, your Social Security benefit will be reduced by $400, two-thirds of the amount of your government pension. Thus, you will end up receiving a $600 monthly annuity payment from CSRS but only $100 from Social Security. Some government pension benefits do not trigger the government pension offset. For more information, see Social Security Administration Publication 05-10007.

VCP: THE CREATIVE SAVINGS SECRET FOR CSRS

> One excellent reason to seek out the services of a financial professional is that he/she spends a huge amount of time learning the ins and outs of all of these retirement programs.

We have a special secret that we like to share with our clients: the CSRS Voluntary Contributions Program (VCP), a special element of the CSRS. Designed to allow CSRS employees to contribute more money and buy an additional retirement annuity, the CSRS VCP program has an additional, and very big, benefit: you can use it to max-fund a Roth IRA. That's extremely good news, especially to service people who thought their incomes were too high to be eligible for a Roth IRA.

Because so few people have heard of the VCP, these are new concepts for most of our clients. So let's look quickly at the VCP and what it means to max-fund a Roth IRA.

How the CSRS VCP can allow you to Max-Fund a Roth IRA

First of all, this is all legitimate. Many people don't think to use the VCP this way, but that's likely because most of our clients haven't even heard of the CSRS Voluntary Contributions Program. It's really not a trick, though. This is just a creative way to use tax law to help our clients achieve the best retirement possible.

Why a Roth IRA?

As we discussed earlier, IRAs are like stickers on cars: the difference between a Traditional and Roth IRA is whether or not your money goes through the tax-deferred tollbooth.

In a Traditional IRA, your money is tax-deferred. By contributing to a Traditional IRA, you're choosing to pay taxes when you take your money out, not when you put it in.

Roth IRAs are the opposite: you pay taxes on your money now, before you put it into the Roth IRA, and if you leave it there the required amount of time, you can withdraw both the principal and interest tax-free.

So, the million dollar questions is, when do you want to pay the taxes?

Tax-deferred accounts are very popular, with a majority of people investing most or all of their retirement money in Traditional IRAs, the TSP, other 401(k)s, etc. That means when they withdraw any of that money during retirement, they will be responsible for paying the taxes on it.

Some people have to consider their federal pensions as well. The majority of FERS and/or CSRS pensions are also taxable. Then there's Social Security as well, which is also taxable.

With that setup, you are responsible for paying taxes on almost your entire retirement savings.

Everybody has to pay taxes. But is it better to pay them now ... or later?

People with tax-deferred accounts are betting that paying taxes later will be the least expensive option. But here's the thing: despite how it may seem, right now, our tax rates are at a historical low. Plus, our government is facing mounting, extreme deficits. Only time will tell, but chances are good that in order to pay those deficits, our government is going to consider raising taxes and raising them significantly.

All of that means one simple thing: pay taxes now, when they are at a historical low, or wait and run the risk of paying at markedly higher tax rates. Taxes are much less likely to go down, since they're already low, and if they DO go up, how will you afford them? With no money coming in during retirement, you'll have to live a diminished lifestyle or perhaps even go back to work ... just to pay those unexpected taxes.

A Roth IRA, however, means that you can take your money out tax free. The taxes will have been paid. And, if you have at least some of your money in a Roth IRA, you can choose where to take your income from if tax rates increase. A Roth IRA puts you in the driver's seat.

But what about those employees who make "too much" income to qualify for a Roth IRA?

> *Roger and Gloria are married and together bring home $200,000 a year. As a result, they're not be eligible to contribute directly to a Roth IRA.*

WWW.PLANNINGASECURERETIREMENT.COM

> *However, Roger and Gloria are federal employees who qualify for the CSRS VCP, which means they have another option. They have savings of $40,000 that they'd like to put in a Roth IRA, but their income level prevents them from contributing even the standard $5,500 or $6,500 a year.*

Then we told them about the CSRS VCP. We helped them open a CSRS VCP and funded it with the $40,000, while also opening a Roth IRA without funding it at all. With just a little paperwork, we had set up to withdraw the $40,000 form their VCP and transfer it to the Roth IRA. It's a roundabout, and totally legitimate, solution that allows Roger and Gloria to protect a significant portion of their retirement from potential tax hikes.

Working with a professional for this kind of little-known information is a great way to find creative solutions to retirement funding, but it's also smart. We can ensure that all of the paperwork and procedures are done correctly, protecting you from possible tax issues in the future.

THE FEDERAL THRIFT SAVINGS PLAN

What is the Federal Thrift Savings Plan (TSP)?

The Federal Thrift Savings Plan (TSP) is a tax-deferred retirement savings and investment plan set up to help federal civilian employees and military personnel (as of October 9, 2001) save for retirement. The Federal Retirement Thrift Investment Board, an independent government agency, administers it. The TSP is a defined contribution plan. This means that employees and service members are eligible to contribute at least part of their salary annually to the plan, and the government may match those contributions in full or in part. Contributions are invested and distributed to the employee or service member at retirement or when the employee or service member separates from government service, or distributed to the employee's or service member's survivors if the employee or servicemember dies.

Who is eligible to participate in the TSP?

Employees covered under the Federal Employees Retirement System (FERS) are automatically enrolled in the TSP by the agency for which they work. Participants may file an election to make contributions to the plan at any time. Elections are effective no later than the first, full pay period after they're received.

Civil Service Retirement System (CSRS) employees are also eligible to contribute a portion of their pay to the TSP, but are generally not entitled to Agency Automatic (1 percent) Contributions and Agency Matching Contributions, as discussed below. Active-duty and reserve members of the Army, Air Force, Marine Corps, Navy, and Coast Guard, as well as uniformed members of the Public Health Service and the National Oceanic and Atmospheric Administration, can also participate by contributing a portion of their pay to the TSP.

CONTRIBUTIONS TO A TSP ACCOUNT

Federal employee's contributions

You can generally contribute up to 100 percent of your basic pay to your thrift account each pay period in 2013, as long as your annual contributions don't exceed the Internal Revenue Code (IRC) elective deferral limit of $17,500. Your contributions reduce your gross income so that you pay less income tax on your earnings. All contributions must be made through payroll deductions. You can elect to contribute to the TSP at any time--there is no waiting period. You may also make Roth contributions to the TSP (see below).

Caution: If you are a FERS employee hired (or a CSRS employee rehired) after July 31, 2010, you will be automatically enrolled the TSP, and 3 percent of your basic pay will be deducted from your paycheck each pay period and deposited in your TSP account, unless you make a contribution election to stop or change your contributions.

Caution: If you participate in another tax-deferred plan, such as a 401(k) or 403(b) plan, your total elective deferrals to all of your plans cannot exceed the $17,500 limit (plus allowable catch-up contributions) in 2013. However, if you also participate in a Section 457(b) plan, your contributions to the TSP are not limited by any of your contributions to your section 457(b) plan.

Tip: Military personnel who receive tax-exempt pay (i.e., combat zone pay) can also contribute some or all of the tax-exempt pay to the TSP. Such contributions will also be tax exempt.

Thrift Savings Plan participants who are age 50 and older can make additional yearly "catch-up" contributions to their TSPs. These contributions can be made over and above the regular contribution limits. The purpose of this provision is to help older plan participants increase their savings as they approach retirement. Those who are age 50 and older can contribute an additional $5,500 to their TSPs in 2013. (The annual catch-up amount is adjusted annually for inflation.)

Caution: Military personnel cannot make catch-up contributions from tax-exempt pay, incentive pay, special pay, or bonus pay.

Roth contributions

Effective May 7, 2012, participants were allowed to designate all or part of their elective deferrals as Roth contributions. Roth contributions are made on an after-tax basis, just like Roth IRA contributions. Unlike pretax contributions to the TSP, there's no up-front tax benefit, but if certain conditions are met, your Roth contributions and earnings are entirely free from federal income tax when distributed from the plan.

Separate accounts are established within TSP (the "Roth accounts") to track each employee's Roth contributions and any gains or losses on those contributions. The taxation of distributions from the Roth account is also determined separately from any other plan dollars.

Government's contributions

If you are covered under FERS, the government contributes an amount equal to 1 percent of the basic pay you earn each pay period to your thrift account whether you contribute a portion of your compensation to the plan or not. These contributions are referred to as Agency Automatic (1 percent) Contributions.

If you are covered under FERS, and elect to contribute a portion of your compensation to the plan, you will also receive Agency Matching Contributions. When you become eligible, your agency will match your contributions up to 5 percent of the basic pay that you contribute each pay period. The first 3 percent of basic pay you contribute is matched dollar-for-dollar, and the remaining 2 percent is matched 50 cents on the dollar.

Example: Naoko was employed under FERS, and a TSP account was automatically opened for her. Her basic pay each pay period was $2,000. Each pay period, the government contributed $20 (1 percent of her basic pay) to her investment account. Naoko contributed $60 (3 percent of her basic pay) each pay period. The government matched her contribution dollar for dollar, so at the end of the year (26 pay periods) Naoko had $3,640 in her TSP account.

We don't recommend doing what Naoko did. The government will match up to 5 percent of your pay.

> **Make sure you take advantage of as much of the free money you can get.**

The TSP is an important pillar of your FERS retirement please make sure you put in the most you can and free money is a great way to do that.

Tip: If you are an employee covered under CSRS or are a service member, the government generally doesn't contribute anything to your plan.

Caution: Although you are always vested in contributions you make to the plan and Agency Matching Contributions (as well as any attributable earnings), most FERS employees are vested in Agency Automatic (1 percent) Contributions only after they have completed three years of federal service. This means that if you leave federal service before you become vested, you won't be entitled to receive any of the automatic contributions or their earnings in your account. However, if you die before becoming vested, all the money in your TSP account will be automatically vested, and your designated beneficiary will be entitled to receive all of the funds in your account.

TSP INVESTMENT OPTIONS

You can invest any percentage of future contributions to your account to a TSP "lifecycle" L Fund, or to any of the five individual funds available. The TSP L Funds are designed for individuals who don't feel comfortable selecting or managing their own investment choices. You simply select the L Fund that's appropriate for your time horizon. The L Fund that you select invests in a mix of the individual funds available under the TSP, and adjusts the mix to reflect a lower tolerance for risk as your investment time horizon approaches.

Instead of an L Fund, you can also invest directly in any or all of the five individual funds offered under the TSP: the Government Securities Investment Fund (G Fund), the Fixed-Income Index Fund (F Fund), the Common Stock Index Investment Fund (C Fund), the small Capitalization Stock Index Invest Fund (S Fund), and the International Stock Index Fund (I Fund).

> **Tip:** Although you can contribute either a percentage of your pay each pay period or a fixed dollar amount to the TSP, you cannot specify that you want a particular dollar amount to go to an individual fund. You can only state what percentage of your contribution you want to go to each fund.

DISTRIBUTION OF TSP ACCOUNT FUNDS

In-service withdrawals

Participants can take a one-time age-based withdrawal from the TSP upon reaching age 59½. All or a portion of the participant's vested account balance may be withdrawn at that time. If a participant elects to take a partial account withdrawal, the participant will not be eligible for a partial account withdrawal upon separating from service.

Participants can also make in-service withdrawals in cases of financial hardship. Specific requirements and limits apply, and each time a participant takes a hardship distribution, the participant is barred from making another hardship distribution for a period of

6 months. In addition, no contributions can be made to the TSP for a 6 month period.

> **Caution:** Participants should consider carefully the consequences of an in-service distribution. Distributions from your pre-tax account are subject to federal income tax, and an additional 10 percent penalty tax will generally apply to distributions made prior to age 59½. The taxation of in-service withdrawals from an employee›s Roth 401(k) account depends on whether the distribution is a qualified or nonqualified withdrawal (discussed in more detail below). Consideration should also be given to the overall depletion of the participant›s retirement savings.

> **Caution:** If you are married, your spouse must be notified of any request for an in-service distribution, and in most cases, must consent.

Partial withdrawals upon separation

If you separate from service, you can take a distribution of $1,000 or more from the TSP, leaving the remaining balance in your account until you decide to withdraw it. You can take only one partial distribution from the account. If you had previously made an aged-based withdrawal after reaching age 59½, you do not have this option.

Full withdrawal upon separation

When you separate from service, you can elect to withdraw your full TSP account in a single "lump-sum" distribution, in a series of specified payments, or through the purchase of an annuity.

You can purchase three types of annuities: (1) an annuity that is paid to you during your lifetime (single life annuity); (2) an annuity that is paid to you while you and your spouse are alive, then paid to the surviving spouse for the rest of his or her life after one of you dies (joint life with spouse annuity); or (3) an annuity that is paid to you while you and a person chosen by you (with an insurable interest in you) are alive, then paid to the survivor (beneficiary) for his or her life after one of you dies. You can also choose certain payment options, depending on the type of annuity you choose, such as a cash refund feature, an increasing benefits option, or a 10-year certain feature. However, if you are a married FERS participant, you must elect a joint life with spouse annuity with a 50 percent survivor benefit, level payments, and no cash refund feature, unless your spouse consents to another annuity option.

> **Tip:** You must have at least $3,500 in your account at the time the TSP uses the money to purchase an annuity; if you don't, you will receive a lump-sum payment.

Annuity payment amounts

Several factors determine how much your monthly annuity payments will be. These factors are as follows: how large your account balance is, the interest rate at the time the TSP purchases your annuity, the performance of your investment fund, your age (and your joint annuitant's age if applicable), and the annuity option you elect. The TSP website (www.tsp.gov) has a calculator you can use to project your future account balance, and you can view tables of approximate annuity payments.

Please look at private sector options before you do any TSP annuity options. There are great options available in the private sector and can be much better for you and your family.

TAX CONSIDERATIONS
Income tax

Money you contribute to your TSP account on a pre-tax basis is taken out of your pay before federal (and most state) taxes are calculated, and investment earnings are tax deferred. Therefore, all of the money in your TSP pre-tax account is taxed as ordinary income when you receive it.

> **Tip:** If you were born before 1936, and receive your entire TSP account balance in a single tax year (a "lump sum distribution") and meet other requirements, you may be able to use a special 10-year tax averaging option to figure your tax.

Income Tax--Roth Contributions

In general
Because your Roth contributions are made on an after-tax basis, there is no up-front tax benefit. They're included in your gross income at the time you contribute to the TSP. And because they're made on an after-tax basis, your Roth contributions are tax-free when distributed from the plan. Investment earnings on your Roth contributions grow tax-deferred while they remain in the plan. Whether they're subject to tax when distributed depends on whether the distribution is qualified or nonqualified.

Qualified distributions
If you receive a qualified distribution from your Roth account, the entire amount distributed, both the Roth contributions and investment earnings, is totally free from federal income tax. A qualified distribution is a payment from your Roth account that meets both of the following requirements:
  • The payment is made after you turn age 59½, become disabled, or die, and

- The payment is made after the end of the five-year period that starts with the year you make your first Roth contributions to the plan

Example(s): Nicole makes her first Roth contribution in December, 2012. 2012 is the first year of Nicole›s five-year waiting period. The five-year waiting period ends on December 31, 2016.

Nonqualified distributions

If a payment doesn't satisfy the conditions for a qualified distribution, the portion of the payment that represents the return of your Roth contributions will still be tax-free, but the portion of the payment that represents earnings on those contributions will be subject to income tax and a potential 10 percent premature distribution tax (unless an exception applies).

A distribution that's made before the five-year waiting period has elapsed will always be a nonqualified distribution. A distribution that's made prior to age 59½, disability, or death (for example, a distribution to upon your termination of employment before attaining age 59½) will also always be a nonqualified distribution.

Tip: IRS proposed regulations provide that each distribution from a Roth 401(k) account is deemed to consist of a pro-rata share of an employee's Roth contributions and investment earnings on those contributions.

Early withdrawal

Any taxable amount paid to you from your TSP account before you reach age 59½ may be subject to a 10 percent premature distribution tax (in addition to the ordinary income tax that you pay on the TSP distribution). However, this additional tax does not apply in certain situations, including the following:

- You separate from government service during or after the calendar year in which you reach age 55
- You choose to receive your account balance as an annuity or in monthly payments based on your life expectancy
- You retire on disability
- The payments are made because of death
- For additional exceptions, see Premature Distribution Rule

Saver's tax credit (tax credit for IRAs and retirement plans)
Certain low- and middle-income taxpayers qualify for the saver's tax credit (also known as the tax credit for IRAs and retirement plans). If you participate in the TSP and meet the income requirements, you may be eligible for a tax credit of up to $1,000 on your federal income tax return for each year you participate in the plan.

QUESTIONS & ANSWERS

Can you borrow money from your TSP?
You may be able to borrow money from your account. However, you'll be expected to repay the loan right away if you leave federal service. The interest you pay will be the G Fund rate in effect at the time your loan application is received. If your loan is considered a general purpose one, you won't be required to document or specify the purpose of your loan. Documentation is required for residential loans only. For more information, contact your personnel office.

Can you roll over an individual retirement account to your TSP?
Whether you are an active or separated federal employee, you can roll over (i.e., transfer) money from a qualified retirement plan or

a traditional IRA to your existing TSP account. Money that you are rolling over must be considered an "eligible rollover distribution" under the IRC. If you are separated from service, you can still roll over money to your TSP account unless you have already made a full withdrawal of your account or are receiving monthly payments.

Can you roll over a distribution from your TSP to another plan?

If you (the plan participant) receive an eligible rollover distribution from your TSP, you may roll over all or part of it to an IRA or to another qualified retirement plan, tax-sheltered annuity plan (Section 403(b) plan), or Section 457 plan. (Special rules apply to TSP distributions received by your beneficiaries following your death.) Special rules apply to rollovers from your Roth account.

CHAPTER 4 RECAP //

- Federal employees hired after Jan. 1, 1984, are covered by FERS, a three-tier retirement system that has unique retirements and benefits.
- Federal employees hired before Jan. 1, 1984, and haven't transferred to FERS, are covered by CSRS.
- The Federal Thrift Savings Plan (TSP) is a tax-deferred retirement savings and investment plan, in which employees are eligible to contribute a portion of their annual salary, contributions that may be matched by the government in full or in part.

5

THE ROTH IRA AND TAX PLANNING

" THE HARDEST THING TO
UNDERSTAND IN THE WORLD IS
THE INCOME TAX.

- Albert Einstein "

Louis Brandeis provides one of the best examples illustrating how tax planning works. Brandeis was Associate Justice on the Supreme Court of the United States from 1916 to 1939. Born in Louisville, Kentucky, Brandeis was an intelligent man with a touch of country charm. He described tax planning this way:

"I live in Alexandria, Virginia. Near the Court Chambers, there is a toll bridge across the Potomac. When in a rush, I pay the dollar toll

and get home early. However, I usually drive outside the downtown section of the city and cross the Potomac on a free bridge.

The bridge was placed outside the downtown Washington, D.C. area to serve a useful social service – getting drivers to drive the extra mile and help alleviate congestion during the rush hour.

If I went over the toll bridge and through the barrier without paying a toll, I would be committing tax evasion.

If I drive the extra mile and drive outside the city of Washington to the free bridge, I am using a legitimate, logical and suitable method of tax avoidance, and I am performing a useful social service by doing so.

*The tragedy is that **few people know that the free bridge exists.**"*

Like Brandeis, most American taxpayers have options when it comes to "crossing the Potomac," so to speak. It's a financial planner's job to tell you what options are available. You can wait until March to file your taxes, at which time you might pay someone to report and pay the government a larger portion of your income. However, you could instead file before the end of the year, work with your financial professional and incorporate a tax plan as part of your overall financial planning strategy. Filing later is like crossing the toll bridge. Tax planning is like crossing the free bridge. Which would you rather do?

The answer to this question is easy. Most people want to save money and pay less in taxes. What makes this situation really difficult in real life, however, is that the signs along the side of the road that direct us to the free bridge are not that clear. To normal Americans, and to plenty of people who have studied it, the U.S. tax code is easy to get lost in. There are all kinds of rules, exceptions to rules, caveats and conditions that are difficult to understand, or even to know about. What you really need to know is your options and the bottom line impacts of those options.

ROTH IRA CONVERSIONS

The attractive qualities of Roth IRAs may have prompted you to explore the possibility of moving some of your assets into a Roth account. Another important difference between the accounts is how they treat Required Minimum Distributions (RMDs). When you turn 70 ½ years old, you are required to take a minimum amount of money out of a traditional IRA. This amount is your RMD. It is treated as taxable income. Roth IRAs, however, do not have RMDs, and their distributions are not taxable. Quite a deal, right?

While having a Roth IRA as part of your portfolio is a good idea, converting assets to a Roth IRA can pose some challenges, depending on what kinds of assets you want to transfer.

One common option is the conversion of a traditional IRA to a Roth IRA. You may have heard about converting your IRA to a Roth IRA, but you might not know the full net result on your income. The main difference between the two accounts is that the growth of investments within a traditional IRA is not taxed until income is withdrawn from the account, whereas taxes are charged on contribution amounts to a Roth IRA, not withdrawals. The problem, however, is that when assets are removed from a traditional IRA, even if the assets are being transferred to a Roth IRA account, taxes apply.

There are a lot of reasons to look at Roth conversions. People have a lot of money in IRAs, up to multiple millions of dollars. Even with $500,000, when they turn 70.5 years old, their RMD is going to be approximately $18,000, and they have to take that out whether they want to or not. It's a tax issue. Essentially, if you will be subject to high RMDs, it could have impacts on how much of your Social Security is taxable, and on your tax bracket.

By paying taxes now instead of later on assets in a Roth IRA, you can realize tax-advantaged growth. You pay once and you're done paying. Your heirs are done paying. It's a powerful tool. Here's a simple example to show you how powerful it can be:

> *Imagine that you pay to convert a traditional IRA to a Roth. You have decided that you want to put the money in a vehicle that gives you a tax-advantaged income option down the road. If you pay a 25 percent tax on that conversion and the Roth IRA then doubles in value over the next 10 years, you could look at your situation as only having paid 12.5 percent tax.*

The prospect of tax-advantaged income is a tempting one. While you have to pay a conversion tax to transfer your assets, you also have turned taxable income into tax free retirement money that you can let grow as long as you want without being required to withdraw it.

There are options, however, that address this problem. Much like the Brandeis story, there may be a "free bridge" option for many investors.

Your financial professional will likely tell you that it is not a matter of whether or not you should perform a Roth IRA conversion, it is a matter of how much you should convert and when.

Here are some of the things to consider before converting to a Roth IRA:

- If you make a conversion before you retire, you may end up paying higher taxes on the conversion because it is likely that you are in some of your highest earning years, placing you in the highest tax bracket of your life. It is possible that a better strategy would be to wait until after you retire, a time when you may have less taxable income, which would place you in a lower tax bracket.
- Many people opt to reduce their work hours from full-time to part-time in the years before they retire. If you

have pursued this option, your income will likely be lower, in turn lowering your tax rate.

- The first years that you draw Social Security benefits can also be years of lower reported income, making it another good time frame in which to convert to a Roth IRA.

One key strategy to handling a Roth IRA conversion is to ***always be able to pay the cost of the tax conversion with outside money***. Structuring your tax year to include something like a significant deduction can help you offset the conversion tax. This way you aren't forced to take the money you need for taxes from the value of the IRA. The reason taxes apply to this maneuver is because when you withdraw money from a traditional IRA, it is treated as taxable income by the IRS. Your financial professional, with the help of the CPAs at their firm, may be able to provide you with options like after-tax money, itemized deductions or other situations that can pose effective tax avoidance options.

Some examples of avoiding Roth IRA conversions taxes include:

- *Using medical expenses that are above 10 percent of your Adjusted Gross Income.* If you have health care costs that you can list as itemized deductions, you can convert an amount of income from a traditional IRA to a Roth IRA that is offset by the deductible amount. Essentially, deductible medical expenses negate the taxes resulting from recording the conversion.
- *Individuals, usually small business owners, who are dealing with a Net Operating Loss (NOL).* If you have NOLs, but aren't able to utilize all of them on your tax return. You can carry them forward to offset the taxable income from the taxes on income you convert to a Roth IRA.
- *Charitable giving.* If you are charitably inclined, you can use the amount of your donations to reduce the amount

of taxable income you have during that year. By matching the amount you convert to a Roth IRA to the amount your taxable income was reduced by charitable giving, you can essentially avoid taxation on the conversion. You may decide to double your donations to a charity in one year, giving them two years' worth of donations in order to off-set the Roth IRA conversion tax on this year's tax return.

- *Investments that are subject to depletion.* Certain investments can kick off depletion expenses. If you make an investment and are subject to depletion expenses, they can be deducted and used to offset a Roth IRA conversion tax.

Not all of the above scenarios work for everyone, and there are many other options for offsetting conversion taxes. The point is that you have options, and your financial professional and tax professional can help you understand those options.

If you have a traditional IRA, Roth conversions are something you should look at. As you approach retirement you should consider your options and make choices that keep more of your money in your pocket, not the government's.

ADDITIONAL TAX BENEFITS OF ROTH IRAS

Not only do Roth IRAs provide you with tax-advantaged growth, they also give you a tax diversified landscape that allows you to maximize your distributions. Chances are that no matter the circumstances, you will have taxed income and other assets subject to taxation. ***But if you have a Roth IRA, you have the unique ability to manage your Adjusted Gross Income (AGI), because you have a tax-advantaged income option!***

Converting to a Roth IRA can also help you preserve and build your legacy. Because Roth IRAs are exempt from RMDs, after you make a conversion from a traditional IRA, your Roth account can grow tax-advantaged for another 15, 20 or 25 years and it can be used as tax-advantaged income by your heirs. It is important to note, however, that non-spousal beneficiaries do have to take RMDs from a Roth IRA, or choose to stretch it and draw tax-advantaged income out of it over their lifetime.

TO CONVERT OR NOT TO CONVERT?

Conversions aren't only for retirees. You can convert at any time. Your choice should be based on your individual circumstances and tax situation. Sticking with a traditional IRA or converting to a Roth, again, depends on your individual circumstances, including your income, your tax bracket and the amount of deductions you have each year.

Is it better to have a Roth IRA or traditional IRA? It depends on your individual circumstance. Some people don't mind having taxable income from an IRA. Their income might not be very high and their RMD might not bump their tax bracket up, so it's not as big a deal. A similar situation might involve income from Social Security. Social Security benefits are taxed based on other income you are drawing. If you are in a position where none or very little of your Social Security benefit is subject to taxes, paying income tax on your RMD may be very easy.

> » *There are also situations where leveraging taxable income from a traditional IRA can work to your advantage come tax time. For example, Michael and Lisa dream of buying a boat when they retire. It is something they have looked forward to their entire marriage. In addition to the savings and investments that they created to supply them with income during retirement, which includes a traditional IRA, they have also saved money for the sole purpose of purchasing a boat once they stop working.*
>
> *When the time comes and they finally buy the boat of their dreams, they pay an additional $15,000 in sales taxes that*

year because of the large purchase. Because they are retired and earning less money, the deductions they used to be able to realize from their income taxes are no longer there. The high amount of sales taxes they paid on the boat puts them in a position where they could benefit from taking taxable income from a traditional IRA.

When Michael and Lisa's financial professional learns about their purchase, he immediately contacts a CPA at his firm to run the numbers. They determine that by taking a $15,000 distribution from their IRA, they could fulfill their income needs to offset the $15,000 sales tax deduction that they were claiming due to the purchase of their boat. In the end, they pay zero taxes on their income distribution from their IRA.

The moral of the story? ***Having a tax diversified landscape gives you options***. Having capital assets that can be liquidated, tax-advantaged income options and sources that can create capital gains or capital losses will put you in a position to play your cards right no matter what you want to accomplish with your taxes. The ace up your sleeve is your financial professional and the CPAs they work with. Do yourself a favor and *plan* your taxes instead of *reporting* them!

CHAPTER 5 RECAP //

- You make more money by saving on taxes than you do by making more money. This simple concept becomes extremely valuable to people in retirement and those living on fixed incomes.

- When you report your taxes, you are paying to record history. When you *plan* your taxes with a financial professional, you are proactively finding the best options for your tax return.

- The future of U.S. taxation is uncertain. You know what the tax rate and landscape is today, but you won't tomorrow. The only thing you can really count on is the trend of increasing taxation.

- Look for the "free bridge" option in your tax strategy.

- Converting from a traditional to a Roth IRA can provide you with tax-advantaged retirement income.

- Converting to a Roth IRA can also help you preserve and build your legacy.

- There are many ways to reduce your taxes. Being smart about your Roth IRA conversion is one of the main ways to do so.

6

RISK & THE COLOR OF MONEY

> THE WAY TO WEALTH, IF YOU DESIRE IT, IS AS PLAIN AS THE WAY TO MARKET. IT DEPENDS CHIEFLY ON TWO WORDS, INDUSTRY AND FRUGALITY; I.E., WASTE NEITHER TIME NOR MONEY, BUT MAKE THE BEST USE OF BOTH.
> *- Benjamin Franklin*

If your investment vehicle is a Lamborghini, and you're closing in on retirement, it's time to rethink the amount of risk you're subjected your nest egg to. But how do you know which money is in what vehicle, and how fast each is going? It helps to think of your money as colors.

For our purposes, Know So Money (which is safer and more dependable) is green. Hope So Money (which is exposed to risk and fluctuates with the market) is red. A financial professional can help you better understand the color of the money in your investment portfolio.

The fact of the matter is that a lot of people don't know their level of exposure to risk. Visually organizing your assets is an important and powerful way to get a clear picture of what kind of money you have, where it is and how you can best use it in the future. This process is as simple as listing your assets and assigning them a color based on their status as Know So or Hope So Money. Work with your financial professional to create a comprehensive inventory of your assets to understand what you are working with before making any decisions. This may be the first time you have ever sat down and sorted out all of your assets, allowing you to see how much money you have at risk in the market. Comparing the color of your investments will give you an idea of how near or far you are from adhering to the Rule of 100.

Over the course of your lifetime, it is likely that you have acquired a variety of assets. Assets can range from money that you have in a savings account or a 401(k), to a TSP or an IRA. You have earned money and have made financial decisions based on the best information you had at the time. When viewed as a whole, however, you might not have an overall strategy for the management of your assets. As we have seen, it's more important than ever to know which of your assets are at risk. High market volatility and low treasury rates make for challenging financial topography. Navigating this financial landscape starts with planful asset management that takes into account your specific needs and options.

Even if you feel that you have plenty of money in your 401(k), IRA or TSP, not knowing how much *risk* those investments are exposed to can cause you major financial suffering. Take the market crash of 2008 for example. In 2008, the average investor lost 30 percent of their 401(k). If more people had shifted their investments away from risk as they neared retirement age (i.e. the Rule of 100), they may have lost a lot less money going into retirement.

When using the Rule of 100 to calculate your level of risk, your financial age might be different than your chronological age, however. The way you organize your assets depends on your goals and your level of comfort with risk. Whatever you determine the appropriate amount of risk for you to be, you will need to organize your portfolio to reflect your goals. If you have more Red Money than Green Money, in particular, you will need to make decisions about how to move it. You can work with a financial professional to find appropriate Green Money options for your situation.

The next step is to know the right amount and ratio of Green and Red Money for you at your stage of retirement planning.

Investing heavily in Red Money and gambling all of your assets on the market is incredibly risky no matter where you fall within the Rule of 100. Money in the market can't be depended on to generate income, and a plan that leans too heavily on Red Money can easily fail, especially when investment decisions are influenced by emotional reactions to market downturns and recoveries. Not only is this an unwise plan, it can be incredibly stressful to an investor who is gambling everything on stocks and mutual funds.

But a plan that uses too much Green Money avoids all volatility and can also fail. Why? Investing all of your money in Certificates of Deposit (CDs), savings accounts, money markets and other low return accounts may provide interest and income, but that likely won't be enough to keep pace with inflation. If you focus exclusively on income from Green Money and avoid owning any

WWW.PLANNINGASECURERETIREMENT.COM

stocks or mutual funds in your portfolio, you won't be able to leverage the potential for long-term growth your portfolio needs to stay healthy and productive. This is where the Rule of 100 can help you determine how much of your money should be invested in the market to anticipate your future needs.

Green Money becomes much more important as you age. While you want to reduce the amount of Red Money you have and to transition it to Green Money, you don't necessarily need all of it to generate income for you right away. Taking a closer look at Green Money, you will see there are actually different types.

TYPES OF GREEN MONEY:
NEED NOW AND NEED LATER

Money that you need to depend on for income is Green Money. Once you have filled the income gap at the beginning of your retirement, you may have money left over.

There are two types of Green Money: money used for income and money used for accumulation to meet your income needs in five, 10 or 20 years. Money needed for income is Need Now Money. It is money you need to meet your basic needs, to pay your bills, your mortgage if you have one and the costs associated with maintaining your lifestyle. Money used for accumulation is Need Later Money. It's money that you don't need now for income, but will need to rely on down the road. It's still Green Money because you will rely on it later for income and will need to count on it being there. Need Later Money represents income your assets will need to generate for future use. When planning your retirement, it is vital to decide how much of your assets to structure for income and how much to set aside to accumulate to create Need Later Money.

You must figure out if your income and accumulation needs are met. Your Need Now and Need Later Money are top priorities. Need Now Money, in particular, will dictate what your options for future needs are.

OPTIMIZING RISK AND FINDING THE RIGHT BALANCE

Determining the amount of risk that is right for you depends on your specific situation. It starts by examining your particular financial position.

The Rule of 100 is a useful way to begin to determine the right amount of risk for you. But remember, it's just a baseline. Use it as a starting point for figuring out where your money should be. If you're a 50-year-old investor, the Rule of 100 suggests that you have 50 percent Green Money and 50 percent Red Money. Most 50-year-olds are more risk tolerant, however. There are many reasons why someone might be more risk tolerant, not the least of which is feeling young! Experienced investors, people who feel they need to gamble for a higher return, or people who have met their retirement income goals and are looking for additional ways to accumulate wealth are all candidates for investment strategies that incorporate higher levels of risk. In the end, it comes down to your personal tolerance for risk. How much are you willing to lose?

> Consulting with a financial professional is often the wisest approach to calculating your risk level.

A professional can help determine your risk tolerance by getting to know you, asking you a set of questions and even giving you a survey to determine your comfort level with different types of risk. Here's a typical scenario a financial professional might pose to you:

"You have $100,000 saved that you would like to invest in the market. There is an investment product that could turn your $100,000

into $120,000. That same option, however, has the potential of losing you up to $30,000, leaving you with $70,000."

Is that a scenario that you are willing to enter into? Or are you more comfortable with this one:

"You could turn your $100,000 into $110,000, but have the potential of losing $15,000, leaving you with $85,000."

Your answer to these and others types of questions will help a financial professional determine what level of risk is right for you. They can then offer you investment strategies and management plans that reflect your financial age.

THE NUMBERS DON'T LIE

When the rubber meets the road, the numbers dictate your options. Your risk tolerance is an important indicator of what kinds of investments you should consider, but if the returns from those investments don't meet your retirement goals, your income needs will likely not be met. For example, if the level of risk you are comfortable with manages your investments at a 4 percent return and you need to realize an 8 percent return, your income needs aren't going to be met when you need to rely on your investments for retirement income. A professional may encourage you to be more aggressive with your investment strategy by taking on more risk in order to give you the potential of earning a greater return. If taking more risk isn't an option that you are comfortable with, then the discussion will turn to how you can earn more money or spend less in order to align your needs with your resources more closely.

How are you going to structure your income flow during retirement? The answer to this question dictates how you determine your risk tolerance. If the numbers say that you need to be more aggressive with your investing, or that you need to modify your lifestyle, it becomes a choice you need to make.

WORKING WITH A FINANCIAL PROFESSIONAL

Take a moment to think about your income goals:

What is your lifestyle today? Would you like to maintain it into retirement? Are you meeting your needs? Are you happy with your lifestyle? What do you really *need* to live on when you retire?

Some people will have the luxury of maintaining or improving their lifestyle, while others may have to make decisions about what they need versus what they want during their retirement.

Organizing your assets, understanding the color of your money, and creating an income and accumulation plan for retirement can quickly become an overwhelming task. The fact of the matter is that financial professionals build their careers around understanding the different variables affecting retirement financing.

Working with a Registered Investment Advisor means working with a professional who is legally obligated to help you make financial decisions that are in your best interest and fall within your comfort zone. Taking steps toward creating a retirement plan is nothing to take lightly. By leveraging tax strategies, properly organizing your assets, and accumulating helpful financial products that help you meet your income and accumulation needs, you are more likely to meet your goals. You might have a million dollars socked away in a savings account, but your neighbor, who has $300,000 in a diverse investment portfolio that is tailored to their needs, may end up enjoying a better retirement lifestyle. Why? They had more than a good work ethic and a penchant for saving. They had a planful approach to retirement asset allocation.

CHAPTER 6 RECAP //

- There are two types of money: Green and Red. Green Money represents assets that are "safer" and more reliable. Red Money represents assets that are exposed to risk.

- There are two types of Green Money: *Need Now and Need Later*. It is important to structure your investments to provide you with income now and later.
- Working with a Registered Investment Advisor will help you compose a clear and concise inventory of your assets, and learn how much they are worth, what rules apply to them, and how they are structured for risk.
- A Registered Investment Advisor can help you structure your investments so as to reflect your risk tolerance.
- Working with an Investment Advisor means working with a professional who is legally obligated to help you make financial decisions that are in your best interest and fall within your comfort zone.

7

THE MEANING OF YELLOW MONEY

> " PEOPLE WHO DON'T RESPECT
> MONEY DON'T HAVE ANY. "
>
> *- J. Paul Getty*

Now that you've calculated the Rule of 100, determined how much risk you have and how much you want, and you've determined how much Green Money you need to meet your short-term and mid-term income needs, it's time to look at what you have left. The money you have left after you've calculated your Green Money needs has the potential of becoming Red Money: your stocks, mutual funds and other investment products that you want to continue accumulating value with the market. You now have the luxury of taking a closer second look at your Red Money to determine how you would like to manage it.

As you will read later in this book in the key findings of the DALBAR report, the deck is stacked against the individual investor. Remember that the average investor on a fixed income failed to keep pace with inflation in nine of the last 14 years, meaning the inherent risk in managing your Red Money is very real and could have a lasting impact on your assets.

So, how much of your Red Money do you invest, and in what kinds of markets, investment products and stocks do you invest? There are a lot of different directions in which you can take your Red Money. One thing is for sure: significant accumulation depends on investing in the market. How you go about doing it is different for everyone. Gathering stocks, bonds and investment funds together in a portfolio without a cohesive strategy behind them could cause you to miss out on the benefits of a more thoughtful and planful approach. The end result is that you may never really understand what your money is doing, where and how it is really invested, and which investment principles are behind the investment products you hold. While you may have goals for each individual piece of your portfolio, it is likely that you don't have a comprehensive plan for your Red Money, which may mean that *you are taking on more risk than you would like, and are getting less return for it than is possible.*

Enter **Yellow Money.** Yellow Money is money that is managed by a professional *with a purpose.* After your income needs are met and you have assets that you would like to dedicate to accumulation, there are decisions you need to make about how to invest those assets. You can buy stocks, index funds, mutual funds, bonds — you name it — you can invest in it. However, the difference between Red Money and Yellow Money is that Yellow Money has a cohesive strategy behind it that is *implemented by a professional.* When you manage your Red Money with an investment plan, it becomes Yellow Money: *money that is being managed with a specific purpose, a specific set of focused goals and a specific strategy in mind.* Yellow Money is still a type of Red Money. It comes with different levels of risk. But Yellow Money is under the watchful eye of professionals who have a stake in the success of your money in the market and who can recommend a range of strategies from those designed for preservation to those targeting rapid growth. You don't want to miss out on achieving the right level of risk, and more importantly, composing a careful plan for the return of your assets.

It can be helpful to think of Red Money and Yellow Money with this analogy:

If you needed to travel through an unfamiliar city in a foreign country, you could rent a car or perhaps hire a driver. Were you to drive yourself, you would try to gain guidance from perplexing road signs and need to adhere to traffic rules – with no experience or assistance to lean on. It would take longer to get to where you want to go, and the chance of a traffic accident would be higher. If you hired a driver, they would manage your journey. A driver would know the route, how to avoid traffic, and follow the rules of the road.

Red Money is like driving yourself. With Yellow Money, you are still traveling by car, but now you have a professional working on your behalf.

CHOOSE AN INVESTMENT STRATEGY YOU BELIEVE IN

Years ago, we took our families to Canada for a fishing trip. We had a great guide who took us salmon fishing, and who was full of knowledge and information about every step of the process. When salmon fishing out at sea with a guide, the guide pretty much does everything but reeling the fish in. There's just something about being there, waiting for a fish to snap the line, and then jumping up and reeling it in.

But there's also risk involved with losing a fish that we did not know about and some we did know about. One of the risks we knew about was not doing a good job reeling in the fish or losing a fish as you try and get it in the boat. Over the first few hours we got 5 fish on the line and only lost one as we were trying to get it in the boat. A risk we did not know about was if we didn't reel in the fish fast enough, a sea lion might jump up and grab it. And then it happened! The line went taut and began to vibrate. We jumped up and grabbed the reel; my son and I were reeling in the biggest salmon of the day...

And the guide grabbed it away from us and started reeling in the fish. He was trying to prevent the possible disappointment of a sea lion stealing our fish, but what he unknowingly stole was the experience of the loss ourselves. We got a great picture on the sea lion jumping out of the water and grabbing our salmon

This is the backbone of our investment philosophy. We can know everything we need to know, and do everything we need to do, and still your investment experience won't be nearly as positive as if we do it together. We want to work together with you teaching you the how and why about saving and investing so we can do it together.

> **We see it as our job to prepare you properly, so that you buy in and become a part of your own investment and savings strategy.**

Investment always involves some degree of risk, and we find that when you're learning and understanding, you feel empowered. It's our goal is to ensure that you never feel like a victim of the market, as so many people do. You will be informed, empowered and involved. And we'll catch some fish, too.

TAKING A CLOSER LOOK AT YOUR PORTFOLIO

Think about your investment portfolio. Think specifically of what you would consider your Red Money. Do you know what is there? You may have several different investment products like individual mutual funds, bond accounts, stocks, etc. You may have inherited a stock portfolio from a relative, or you might be invested in a bond account offered by the company for which you worked due to your familiarity with them. While you may or may not be managing your investments individually, the reality is that you probably don't have an overall management strategy for all of your investments. Investments that aren't managed are simply Red Money, or money that is at risk in the market. Harnessing the earning potential of your Red Money relies on more than a collection of stocks and bonds, however. It needs guided management. A good Yellow Money manager uses the knowledge they have about the level of risk with which you are comfortable, what you need or want to use your money for, when you want or need it and how you want to use it. The Yellow Money objects that they choose for you will still have a certain level of risk, but under the right management, control and process, you have a far better chance of a successful outcome that meets your specific needs.

When you sit down with an investment professional, you can look at all of your assets together. Chances are that you have accumulated a number of different assets over the last 20, 30 or 50 years. You may have a put a 401(k), TSP, an IRA, a Roth IRA, sticker on your saving vehicles or you might have an account of self-directed stocks, a brokerage account, etc. Wherever you put your money, a financial professional will go through your assets and help you determine the level of risk to which you are exposed now and should be exposed in the future.

Here is a typical example of how an investment professional can be helpful to a future retiree with Yellow Money needs:

> » *Susan is 65 years old and wants to retire in two years. She has a 401(k) from her job to which she has contributed*

for 26 years. She also has some stocks that her late husband managed. Susan also has $55,000 in a mutual fund that her sister recommended to her five years ago and $30,000 in another mutual fund that she heard about at work. She takes a look at her assets one day and decides that she doesn't understand what they add up to or what kind of retirement they will provide. She decides to meet with an investment professional.

Janet's professional immediately asks her:

Does she know exactly where all of her money is? Susan doesn't know much about all her husband's stocks, which have now become hers. Their value is at $100,000 invested in three large cap companies. Janet is unsure of the companies and whether she should hold or sell them.

Does she know what types of assets she owns? Yes and no. She knows she had 401(k) and IRA stickers on some assets, but she is unfamiliar with her husband's self-directed stock portfolio or the type of mutual funds she owns as vehicles with the 401(k) and IRA stickers on them. Furthermore she is unclear as to how to manage the holdings as she nears retirement. She does not know how to create income for her daily needs.

Does she know the strategies behind each one of the investment products she owns? While Susan knows she had a 401(k), an IRA and mutual fund holdings, she doesn't know how her 401(k) is invested or how to make it more conservative as she nears retirement. She is unsure whether her IRA is a Roth or traditional variety and how to draw income from them. She really does not have specific investment principles guiding her investment decisions, and she doesn't know anything about her husband's individual stocks. One major concern for Susan is whether her family would be okay if she were not around.

After determining Susan's assets, her financial professional prepares a consolidated report that lays out all of her assets for her to review. Her professional explains each one of them to her. Susan discovers that although she is two years away from retiring, her 401(k) is invested with an amount of risk with which she is not comfortable. Her 401(k) vehicle is a Porsche and she does not like driving the Porsche this close to retirement. She wants something that matches her daily needs. Sixty percent of her 401(k) is at risk, far off the mark if we abide by the Rule of 100. Janet opts to be more conservative than the Rule of 100 suggests, as she will rely on her 401(k) for most of her immediate income needs after retirement. Susan's professional also points out several instances of overlap between her mutual funds. Susan learns that while she is comfortable with one of her mutual funds, she does not agree with the management principles of the other. In the end, Susan's professional helps her re-organize her 401(k) to secure her more Green Money for retirement income. Her professional also uses her mutual fund and her husband's stock assets to create a growth oriented investment plan that Janet will rely on for Need Later Money in 15 years when she plans on relocating closer to her children and grandchildren. By creating an overall investment strategy, Susan is able to meet her targeted goals in retirement. Susan's financial professional worked closely with her and her tax professional to minimize the tax impact of any asset sales on Janet's situation.

Like Susan, you may have several savings vehicles with different stickers on them: a 401(k), an IRA or a TSP to which you regularly contribute, some mutual funds to which you make monthly contributions, etc. But what is your *overall investment strategy*? Do you have one in place? Do you want one that will help you meet your retirement goals? Yellow Money looks at *ALL* your accounts

WWW.PLANNINGASECURERETIREMENT.COM

and all their different strategies to create a plan that helps them all work together. Your current investment situation may not reflect your wishes. As a matter of fact, it likely doesn't.

You may have a better understanding of your assets than Janet did, but even someone with an investment strategy can benefit from having a financial professional review their portfolio:

> » John is 69 years old. He retired four years ago. He relied on income from an IRA for three years in order to increase his Social Security benefit. He also made significant investments in 36 different mutual funds. He chose to diversify among the funds by selecting a portion for growth, another for good dividends, another that focused on promising small cap companies and a final portion that work like index funds. All the money that John had in mutual funds he considered Need Later Money that he wanted to rely on in his 80s. After the stock market took a hit in 2008, John lost some confidence in his investments and decided to sit down with a financial professional to see if his portfolio was able to recover.
>
> The professional John met with was able to determine what goals he had in mind. Specifically, the financial professional determined what John actually wanted and needed the money for, and when he needed it. His professional also looked inside each of the mutual funds and discovered several instances of overlap. While John had created diversity in his portfolio by selecting funds focused on different goals, he didn't account for overlap in the companies in which the funds were invested. Out of the 36 funds, his professional found that 20 owned nearly identical stock. While most of the companies were good investments, the high instance of overlap did not contribute to the healthy investment diversity that John wanted.
>
> John's professional consolidated his assets into one investment management strategy. This allowed John's investments

to be managed by someone he trusted who knew his specific investment goals and needs. Eliminating redundancy and overlap in his portfolio was easy to do but difficult to detect since John had multiple funds with multiple brokerage firms. John sat down with a professional to see if his mutual funds could perform well, and he left with a consolidated management plan and a money manager who understood him personally. That's Yellow Money at its best.

AVOIDING EMOTIONAL INVESTING

There's no way around it; people get emotional about their money and for good reason. You've spent your life working for it, exchanging your time and talent for it, and making decisions about how to invest it, save it and make it grow. The maintenance of your lifestyle and your plans for retirement all depend on it. The best investment strategies, however, don't rely on emotions. One of Yellow Money's greatest strengths lies in the fact that it is managed by someone who understands your needs and desires, but doesn't make decisions about your money under the influence of emotion.

A well-managed investment account meets your goals as a whole, not in individualized and piecemeal ways. Professional money managers do this by creating requirements for each type of investment in which they put your money. We'll call them "screens." Your money manager will run your holdings through the screens they have created to evaluate different types of investment strategies. A professionally managed account will only have holdings that meet the requirements laid out in the overall management plan that was designed to meet your investment goals. The holdings that don't make it through the screens, the ones that don't contribute to your investment goals, are sold and redistributed to investments that your financial professional has determined to be appropriate.

Different screens apply to different Yellow Money strategies. For example, if one of your goals is significant growth, which would require taking on more risk alongside the potential for more return, an investment professional would screen for companies that have high rates of revenue and sales growth, high earnings growth, rising profit margins, and innovative products. On the other hand, if you want your portfolio to be used for income, which would call for lower risk and less return, your professional would screen for dividend yield and sector diversification. *Every investor has a different goal, and every goal requires a customized strategy that uses quantitative screens.* A professional will create a portfolio that reflects your investment desires. If some of the current assets you own complement the strategies that your professional recommends, those will likely stay in your portfolio.

Screening your assets removes emotions from the equation. It removes attachment to underperforming or overly risky investments. Financial professionals aren't married to particular stocks or mutual funds for any reason. They go by the numbers and see your portfolio through a lens shaped by your retirement goals. Your professional understands your wants and needs, and creates an investment strategy that takes your life events and future plans into account. It's a planful approach, and it allows you to tap into the tools and resources of a professional who has built a career around successful investing. Managing money is a full time job and is best left to a professional money manager.

Removing emotions from investing also allows you to be unaffected by the day-to-day volatility of the market. Your financial professional doesn't ask where the market is going to be in a year, three years or a month from now. If you look at the value of the stock market from the beginning of the twentieth century to today, it's going up. Despite the Great Depression, despite the 1987 crash, despite the 2008 market downturn, the market, as a whole, trends up.

WWW.PLANNINGASECURERETIREMENT.COM

> **Remember the major market downturn in 2008 when the market lost 30 percent of its value?**

Not only did it completely recover, it has far exceeded its 2008 value. Emotional investing led countless people to sell low as the market went down, and buy the same shares back when the market started to recover. That's an expensive way to do business. While you can't afford to lose money that you need in two, three or five years, your Need Later Money has time to grow. The best way to do so is to make it Yellow.

CREATING AN INVESTMENT STRATEGY

Just like Susan and John, chances are that you can benefit from taking a more managed investment approach tailored to your goals. Yellow Money is generally Need Later Money that you want to grow for needs you'll have in at least 10 years. You can work with your financial planner to create investments that meet your needs within different timeframes. You may need to rely on some of your Yellow Money in 10, 15 or 20 years, whether for additional income, a large purchase you plan on making or a vacation. Whatever you want it for, you will need it down the road. A financial professional can help you rescale the risk of your assets as they grow, helping you lock in your profits and secure a source of income you can depend on later.

So what does a Yellow Money account look like? Here's what it *does not* look like: a portfolio with 49 small cap mutual funds, a dozen individual stocks and an assortment of bond accounts. A brokerage account with a hodgepodge of investments, even if goal-oriented, is not a professionally managed account. It's still Red Money. Remember, Yellow Money is a managed account that has an overarching investment philosophy. When you look at making investments that will perform to meet your future income needs, the burning question becomes: How much should you have in the market and how should it be invested? Working with a professional will help you determine how much risk you should take, how to balance your assets so they will meet your goals and how to plan for the big ticket items, like health care expenses, that may be in your future. Yes, Yellow Money is exposed to risk, but by working with a professional, you can manage that risk in a productive way.

WHY YELLOW MONEY?

If you have met your immediate income needs for retirement, why bother with professionally managing your other assets? The money you have accumulated above and beyond your income needs probably has a greater purpose. It may be for your children or grandchildren. You may want to give money to a charity or organization that you admire. It may be needed to grow and add to your lifestyle in retirement. In short, you may want to craft your legacy or increase your enjoyment of retirement.. It would be advantageous to grow your assets in the best manner possible would it not? A financial professional has built a career around managing money in profitable ways. They are experts and understand how to protect their clients from risk of loss; maximizing growth and how to outpace inflation.

Turning to Yellow Money also means that you don't have to burden yourself with the time commitment, the stress, and the cost of determining how to manage your money. Yellow Money can help you better enjoy your retirement. Do you want to sit down in your home office every day and determine how to best allocate your assets, or do you want to be living your life while someone else manages your money for you? When the majority of your Red Money is managed with a specific purpose by a financial professional, you don't have to be worrying about which stocks to buy and sell today or tomorrow. The power of Yellow Money is the same as using a professional to fix your car, home electrical or plumbing it can save you from having huge headaches in retirement.

SEEKING FINANCIAL ADVICE: STOCK BROKERS VS. INVESTMENT ADVISOR REPRESENTATIVES

Investors basically have access to two types of advice in today's financial world: advice from stock brokers and advice given by investment advisors. Most investors, however, don't know the difference between types of advice and the people from whom they receive advice. Today, there are two primary types of advice offered to investors: advice given by a commission-based registered representative (brokers) and advice given by fee-based Investment Advisor Representatives. Unfortunately, many investors are not aware that a difference exists; nor have they been explained the distinction between the two types of advice. In a survey taken by TD Ameritrade, the top reasons investors choose to work with an independent registered investment advisor are:*

- Registered Investment Advisors are required, as fiduciaries, to offer advice that is in the best interest of clients.
- More personalized service and competitive fee structure offered at a Registered Investment Advisor firm.
- Dissatisfaction with full commission brokers.

The truth is that there is a great deal of difference between stock brokers and investment advisor representatives. For starters, investment advisor representatives are obligated to act in an investor's best interests in all aspects of a financial relationship. Confusion continues to exist among investors struggling to find

*2011 Advisor Sentiment Study, commissioned by TD AMERITRADE. TD Ameritrade, Inc.

the best financial advice out there and the most credible sources of advice.

Here is some information to help clear up the confusion so you can find good advice from a professional you can trust:

Investment advisor representatives have the fiduciary duty to act in a client's best interest at all times with every investment decision they make. Stock brokers and brokerage firms usually do not act as fiduciaries to their investors and are not obligated to make decisions that are entirely in the best interest of their customers. For example, if you decide you want to invest in precious metals, a stock broker would offer you a precious metals account from their firm. An Investment Advisor would find you a precious metals account that is the best fit for you based on the investment strategy of your portfolio.

Investment advisors give their clients a Form ADV describing the methods that the professional uses to do business. An Investment Advisor also obtains client consent regarding any conflicts of interest that could exist with the business of the professional.

Stock brokers and brokerage firms are not obligated to provide comparable types of disclosure to their customers.

Whereas stock brokers and firms routinely earn large profits by trading as principal with customers, Investment Advisors cannot trade with clients as principal (except in very limited and specific circumstances).

Investment Advisors charge a pre-negotiated fee with their clients in advance of any transactions. They cannot earn additional profits or commissions from their customers' investments without prior consent. Registered Investment Advisors are commonly paid an asset-based fee that aligns their interests with those of their clients. Brokerage firms and stock brokers, on the other hand, have much different payment agreements. Their revenues may increase regardless of the performance of their customers' assets.

Unlike brokerage firms, where investment banking and underwriting are commonplace, Registered Investment Advisors must manage money in the best interests of their customers. Because Registered Investment Advisors charge set fees for their services, their focus is on their client. Brokerage firms may focus on other aspects of the firm that do not contribute to the improvement of their clients' assets.

Unlike brokers, Registered Investment Advisors do not get commissions from fund or insurance companies for selling their investment products.

Just to drive home the point, here is what a fiduciary duty to a client means for a Registered Investment Advisor. Registered Investment Advisors must:*

- Always act in the best interest of their client and make investment decisions that reflect their goals.
- Identify and monitor securities that are illiquid.
- When appropriate, employ fair market valuation procedures.
- Observe procedures regarding the allocation of investment opportunities, including new issues and the aggregation of orders.
- Have policies regarding affiliated broker-dealers and maintenance of brokerage accounts.
- Disclose all conflicts of interest.
- Have policies on use of brokerage commissions for research.
- Have policies regarding directed brokerage, including step-out trades and payment for order flow.
- Abide by a code of ethics.

---

*2011 Advisor Sentiment Study, commissioned by TD AMERITRADE. TD Ameritrade, Inc.

CHAPTER 7 RECAP //

- Yellow Money may make Red Money less dangerous.
- Yellow Money is professionally managed.
- Yellow Money has a cohesive purpose and a strategy behind it.
- If you haven't sat down and thought about how much money you need in order to generate income during retirement, you're just speculating.
- Red Money is like driving yourself in unfamiliar territory. With Yellow Money, you are still traveling by car, but now you have a professional driving on your behalf.
- The deck is stacked against the ordinary investor. According to the DALBAR report, discussed later in this book, individual investors consistently underperform compared to the market because of a variety of factors, including emotional investing.
- Yellow Money is managed without emotions.
- Checking your truly Red Money should be like checking the sports section. You are interested in it, but it won't directly affect your lifestyle. If your Red Money goes down 50 percent, no one should have to scrape you off the floor.

PART TWO:
PLAN YOUR RETIREMENT DREAM

Retirement age is different for everyone. Some public employees are eligible for retirement as early as when they reach 30 years of service, regardless of their age, while the minimum age to draw Social Security as a retiree is 62. Retirement age depends on how much you like the work you do, and how capable your body is of continuing to do it. Only you can determine what will be the right age for you, but it's good to have not just an idea of when that will be, but also a plan should circumstances demand that you retire earlier.

For the purposes of this book, we're going to say that about 10-15 years before you want to retire, you should start putting your plans into motion. You might have met with a financial advisor once before this, or even better, once every few years or more often. But now, it's time to start seeing your financial team regularly and ensuring that each piece of your retirement plan is falling into place. Changing laws, such as inheritance or income tax laws, could alter plans that you previously made. So now is the time to be vigilant and involved, even if you've taken a relaxed approach to your retirement plans until now.

8
THE BUILDING BLOCKS OF YOUR INCOME PLAN

> " IF SAVING MONEY IS WRONG, I
> DON'T WANT TO BE RIGHT! "
>
> *- William Shatner*

An important aspect of your financial plan is the evaluation of your income needs. Finding the most efficient and beneficial way to address them will have impacts on your lifestyle, your asset accumulation and your legacy planning after you retire. When you have identified your income need, you will know how much to structure for income and how much to be set aside for accumulation.

Every financial strategy for retirement needs first to accommodate the day-to-day need for income. The moment your working income ceases and you start living off the money you've set aside for retirement is referred to as the **retirement cliff.** When you begin drawing income from your retirement assets, you have entered the distribution phase of your financial plan. *The distribution phase of your retirement plan* is when you reach the point of relying on your assets for income. This is where your Green Money comes into play: the safer, more reliable assets that you have accumulated that are designed to provide you with a steady income. On day one of your retirement, you will need a steady and reliable supply of income from your Green Money.

Satisfying that need for daily income entails first knowing *how much you need* and *when you will need it.*

How Much Money Do You Need? While this amount will be different for everyone, the general rule of thumb is that a retiree will require 70 to 80 percent of their pre-retirement income to maintain their lifestyle. Once you know what that number is, the key becomes matching your income need with the correct investment strategies, options and tools to satisfy that need.

When Do You Need Your Money? If you need income to last 10 years, use a tool that creates just that. If you need a lifetime of income, seek a tool that will do that and won't run out.

So how do you figure out how much you need and when you need it? When you take health care costs, potential emergencies, plans for moving or traveling, and other retirement expenses into account, you can really give your calculator a workout. You want to maximize retirement benefits to meet your lifetime income needs. An Investment Advisor can help you answer those questions by working with you to customize an income plan.

As we determined earlier in Chapter 1, the most important thing you need to do as you create an income plan is to take care to avoid too much exposure to risk. You can start by meeting with an Investment Advisor to organize your assets. Get your Green Money and Red Money in order and balanced to meet your needs. If the market goes down 18 percent this afternoon, you don't want that to come out of what you're relying on for next year's income. Hot on the heels of securing your Green Money, it's time to structure those Green Money assets so they can generate income for you. Ultimately, you have to take care of your monthly income needs to pay the bills.

The Big Kahuna of Green Money is your Social Security benefit.

CHAPTER 8 RECAP //

- The foundation of a retirement strategy depends on knowing how much money you need and when you need it.

9

MAKING SENSE OF
SOCIAL SECURITY

One kind of Green Money that most Americans can rely on for income when they retire is Social Security. If you're like most Americans, Social Security is or will be an important part of your retirement income and one that you should know how to properly manage. As a first step in creating your income plan, a financial professional will take a look at your Social Security benefit options. Social Security is the foundation of income planning for anyone who is about to retire and is a reliable source of Green Money in your overall income plan.

» *William, 63 and Linda, 62, retired this past June. Before they retired, however, we had been working with them for many years to get ready for this transition. Part of that work had been to run the numbers and determine the best time to*

WWW.PLANNINGASECURERETIREMENT.COM

> start filing for each of their Social Security benefits. We discovered that William's Social Security comes in at $1,800 a month if he starts collecting at the end of year, but Linda's, if she begins collecting at the same time, is only about $1000 a month. So, if Linda and William use half his Social Security amount to determine Linda's amount from age 62 till age 66, and defer her filing on her Social Security for four years (to age 66), they'd be living, (but not solely), on $2,700 a month. And there's a good reason to do it! In JUST FOUR YEARS, her Social Security payment will increase to $1,400 a month. That means by giving up $100 a month now for next four years, she will get $400 a month more for the rest of her life. If she just knows those numbers, she can make an informed decision and increase the amount she will receive over her lifetime from Social Security.

Sadly, you can't simply rely on calling Social Security to get this sort of analysis. First of all, Social Security employees are only authorized to answer *the questions you know to ask.* What's more, an overwhelming number of Social Security employees are retiring. In fact, 50 percent of all federal employees are eligible for retirement within the next five years. So, even if you call, your chances of getting an experienced employee who knows the system are very small. Now, more than ever, you need to consult a financial professional before making your Social Security decisions.

Here are some facts that illustrate how Americans currently use Social Security:

- 90 percent of Americans age 65 and older receive Social Security benefits.*
- Social Security provides 39 percent of income for retired Americans.*

*http://www.ssa.gov/pressoffice/basicfact.htm

- Claiming Social Security benefits at the wrong time can reduce your monthly benefit by up to 57 percent.**
- 43 percent of men and 48 percent of women claim Social Security benefits at age 62.**
- 74 percent of retirees receive reduced Social Security benefits.**
- In 2013, the average monthly Social Security benefit was $1,261. *The maximum benefit for 2013 was $2,533. The $1,272 monthly benefit reduction between the average and the maximum is applied for life.****

> **There are many aspects of Social Security that are well known and others that aren't.**

When it comes time for you to cash in on your Social Security benefit, you will have many options and choices. Social Security is a massive government program that manages retirement benefits for millions of people. Experts spend their entire careers understanding and analyzing it. Luckily, you don't have to understand all of the intricacies of Social Security to maximize its advantages. You simply need to know the best way to manage your Social Security benefit. You need to know exactly what to do to get the most from your Social Security benefit and when to do it. Taking the time to create a roadmap for your Social Security strategy will help ensure that you are able to exact your maximum benefit and efficiently coordinate it with the rest of your retirement plan.

There are many aspects of Social Security that you have no control over. You don't control how much you put into it, and you don't control what it's invested in or how the government manages it. However, you do control when and how you file for

---

**When to Claim Social Security Benefits, David Blanchett, CFA, CFP® January, 2013*

****http://www.socialsecurity.gov/pressoffice/factsheets/colafacts2013.com*

benefits. The real question about Social Security that you need to answer is, "When should I start taking Social Security?" While this is the all-important question, there are a couple of key pieces of information you need to track down first.

Before we get into a few calculations and strategies that can make all the difference, let's start by covering the basic information about Social Security which should give you an idea of where you stand. Just as the foundation of a house creates the stable platform for the rest of the framework to rest upon, your Social Security benefit is an important part of your overall retirement plan. The purpose of the information that follows is not to give an exhaustive explanation of how Social Security works, but to give you some tools and questions to start understanding how Social Security affects your retirement and how you can prepare for it. Let's start with eligibility.

Eligibility. Understanding how and when you are eligible for Social Security benefits will help clarify what to expect when the time comes to claim them.

To receive retirement benefits from Social Security, you must earn eligibility. In almost all cases, Americans born after 1929 must earn 40 quarters of credit to be eligible to draw their Social Security retirement benefit. In 2013, a Social Security credit represents $1,160 earned in a calendar quarter. The number changes as it is indexed each year, but not drastically. In 2012, a credit represented $1,130. Four quarters of credit is the maximum number that can be earned each year. In 2013, an American would have had to earn at least $4,640 to accumulate four credits. In order to qualify for retirement benefits, you must earned a minimum number of credits. Additionally, if you are at least 62 years old and have been married to a recipient of Social Security benefits for at least 12 months, you can choose to receive Spousal Benefits. Although 40 is the minimum number of credits required to begin drawing benefits, it is important to know that once you claim your Social Security benefit, there is no going back. Although there may be cost of living adjustments made, you are locked into that base benefit amount forever.

Primary Insurance Amount. You can think of your Primary Insurance Amount (PIA) like a ripening fruit. It represents the amount of your Social Security benefit at your Full Retirement Age (FRA). Your benefit becomes fully ripe at your FRA, and will neither reduce nor increase due to early or delayed retirement options. If you opt to take benefits before your FRA, however, your monthly benefit will be less than your PIA. You will essentially be picking an unripened fruit. On the one hand, waiting until after your FRA to access your benefits will increase your benefit beyond your PIA. On the other hand, you don't want the fruit to overripen, because every month you wait is one less check you get from the government.

Full Retirement Age. Your FRA is an important figure for anyone who is planning to rely on Social Security benefits in their retirement. Depending on when you were born, there is a specific age at which you will attain FRA. Your FRA is dictated by your year of birth and is the age at which you can begin your full monthly benefit. Your FRA is important because it is half of the equation used to calculate your Social Security benefit. The other half of the equation is based on when you start taking benefits.

When Social Security was initially set up, the FRA was age 65, and it still is for people born before 1938. But as time has passed, the age for receiving full retirement benefits has increased. If you were born between 1938 and 1960, your full retirement age is somewhere on a sliding scale between 65 and 67. Anyone born in 1960 or later will now have to wait until age 67 for full benefits. Increasing the FRA has helped the government reduce the cost of the Social Security program, which pays out more than a half trillion dollars to beneficiaries every year!*

While you can begin collecting benefits as early as age 62, the amount you receive as a monthly benefit will be less than it would be if you wait until you reached your FRA or surpass your FRA. It is important to note that if you file for Social Security benefit before your FRA, *the reduction to your monthly benefit will remain in place for the rest of your life.* You can also delay receiving benefits up to age 70, in which case your benefits will be higher than your PIA for the rest of your life.

At FRA, 100 percent of PIA is available as a monthly benefit.

At age 62, your Social Security retirement benefits are available. For each month you take benefits prior to your FRA, however, the monthly amount of your benefit is reduced. *This reduction stays in place for the rest of your life.*

At age 70, your monthly benefit reaches its maximum. After you turn age 70, your monthly benefit will no longer increase.

Year of Birth	Full Retirement Age
1943-1954	66
1955	66 and 2 months
1956	66 and 4 months
1957	66 and 6 months
1958	66 and 8 months
1959	66 and 10 months
1960 or later	age 67*

ROLLING UP YOUR SOCIAL SECURITY

Your Social Security income "rolls up" the longer you wait to claim it. Your monthly benefit will continue to increase until you turn 70 years old. But because Social Security is the foundation of most people's retirement, many Americans feel that they don't have control over how or when they receive their benefits. As a

---

* *http://www.ssa.gov/OACT/progdata/nra.html*

matter of fact, only 4 percent of Americans wait until after their FRA to file for benefits! This trend persists, despite the fact that every dollar you increase your Social Security income by means less money you will have to spend from your nest egg to meet your retirement income needs! For many people, creating their Social Security strategy is the most important decision they can make to positively impact their retirement. *The difference between the best and worst Social Security decision can be tens of thousands of dollars over a lifetime of benefits — up to $170,000!*

Deciding NOW or LATER: Following the above logic, it makes sense to wait as long as you can to begin receiving your Social Security benefit. However, the answer isn't always that simple. Not everyone has the option of waiting. Many people need to rely on Social Security on day one of their retirement. In fact, *nearly 50 percent of 62-year-old Americans file for Social Security benefits.* Why is this number so high? Some might need the income. Others might be in poor health and don't feel they will live long enough to make waiting until reaching FRA worthwhile for themselves or their families. It is also possible, however, that the majority of folks taking an early benefit at age 62 are simply under-informed about Social Security. Perhaps they make this major decision based on rumors and emotion.

File Immediately if You:
- Find your job is unbearable.
- Are willing to sacrifice retirement income.
- Are not healthy and need a reliable source of income.

Consider Delaying Your Benefit if You:
- Want to maximize your retirement income.
- Want to increase retirement benefits for your spouse.
- Are still working and like it.
- Are healthy and willing / able to wait to file.

So if you decide to wait, how long should you wait? Lots of people can put it off for a few years, but not everyone can wait until they are 70 years old. Your individual circumstances may be able to help you determine when you should begin taking Social Security. If you do the math, you will quickly see that between ages 62 and 70, there are 96 months in which you can file for your Social Security benefit. If you take into account those 96 months and the 96 months your spouse could also file for Social Security, the number of different strategies for structuring your benefit, you can easily end up with more than 20,000 different scenarios. It's safe to say this isn't the kind of math that most people can easily handle. Each month would result in a different benefit amount. The longer you wait, the higher your monthly benefit amount becomes. Each month you wait, however, is one less month that you receive a Social Security check.

The goal is to maximize your lifetime benefits. That may not always mean waiting until you can get the largest monthly payment. Taking the bigger picture into account, you want to find out how to get the most money out of Social Security over the number of years that you draw from it. Don't underestimate the power of optimizing your benefit: the difference between the BEST and WORST Social Security election can easily be between $30,000 to $50,000 in lifetime benefits. *The difference can be very substantial!*

If you know that every month you wait, your Social Security benefit goes up a little bit, and you also know that every month you wait, you receive one less benefit check, how do you determine where the sweet spot is that maximizes your benefits over your lifetime? Financial professionals have access to software that will calculate the best year and month for you to file for benefits based on your default life expectancy. You can further customize that information by estimating your life expectancy based on your health, habits and family history. If you can then create an income plan (we'll get into this later in the chapter) that helps you wait until the target date for you to file for Social Security, you can optimize your retirement income strategy to get the most out of your Social Security benefit. How can you calculate your life expectancy? Well, you don't know exactly how long you'll live, but you have a better idea than the government does. They rely on averages to make their calculations. *You have much more personal information about your health, lifestyle and family history than they do.* You can use that knowledge to game the system and beat all the other people who are making uninformed decisions by filing early for Social Security.

While you can and should educate yourself about how Social Security works, the reality is you don't need to know a lot of general information about Social Security in order to make choices about your retirement. What you do need to know is exactly *what to do to maximize your benefit.* Because knowing what you need to do has huge impacts on your retirement! For most Americans, Social Security is the foundation of income planning for retirement. Social Security benefits represent nearly 40 percent of the income of retirees.* For many people, it can represent the largest portion of their retirement income. Not treating your Social Security benefit as an asset and investment tool can lead to sub-optimization of your largest source of retirement income.

Despite the importance of knowing when and how to take your Social Security benefit, many of today's retirees and pre-retirees may know little about the mechanics of Social Security and how they can maximize their benefit.

So, to whom should you turn for advice when making this complex decision? Before you pick up the phone and call Uncle Sam, you should know that the Social Security Administration (SSA) representatives are actually prohibited from giving you

*http://www.socialsecurity.gov/pressoffice/basicfact.htm

election advice! Plus, SSA representatives in general are trained to focus on monthly benefit amounts, not the lifetime income for a family.

MAXIMIZING YOUR LIFETIME BENEFIT

Calculating how to maximize your **lifetime benefits** is more important than waiting until age 70 for your maximum **monthly benefit amount.** It's about getting the most income during your lifetime. Professional benefit maximization software can target the year and month that it is most beneficial for you to file based on your life expectancy.

The three most common ages that people associate with retirement benefits are 62 (Earliest Eligible Age), 66 (Full Retirement Age), and 70 (age at which monthly maximum benefit is reached). In almost all circumstances, however, none of those three most common ages will give you the maximum lifetime benefit.

Remember, every month you wait to file, the amount of your benefit check goes up, but you also get one less check. You don't know how exactly how long you're going to live, but you have a better idea of your life expectancy than the actuaries at the Social Security Administration who can only work with averages. They can't make calculations based on your specific situation. A professional can run the numbers for you and get the target date that maximizes your potential lifetime benefits. You can't get this information from the SSA, but you *can* get it from a financial professional.

Your Social Security options don't stop here, however. There are a plethora of other choices you can make to manipulate your benefit payments.

Just a Few Types of Social Security Benefits:

Retired Worker Benefit. This is the benefit with which most people are familiar. The Retired Worker Benefit is what most people are talking about when they refer to Social Security. It is your benefit based on your earnings and the amount that you have paid into the system over the span of your career.

Spousal Benefit. The Spousal Benefit is available to the spouse of someone who is eligible for Retired Worker Benefits. What if there was a way for your spouse to receive his or her benefit for four years and not lose the chance to get his or her maximum benefit when he or she turns age 70? Many people do not know about this strategy and might be missing out on benefits they have earned.

Survivorship Benefit. When one spouse passes away, the survivor is able to receive the larger of the two benefit amounts.

File and Suspend. This concept allows for a lower-earning spouse to receive up to 50 percent of the other's PIA amount if both spouses file for benefits at the right time.

Restricted Application. A higher-earning spouse may be able to start collecting a spousal benefit on the lower-earning spouse's benefit while allowing his or her benefit to continue to grow.

THE DIVORCE FACTOR

How does a divorced spouse qualify for benefits? If you have gone through a divorce, it might affect the retirement benefit to which you are entitled.

A person can receive benefits as a divorced spouse on a former spouse's Social Security record if he or she:

- Was married to the former spouse for at least 10 years;
- Is at least age 62 years old;
- Is unmarried; and
- Is not entitled to a higher Social Security benefit on his or her own record.*

---

*http://www.ssa.gov/retire2/yourdivspouse.htm

With all of the different options, strategies and benefits to choose from, you can see why filing for Social Security is more complicated than just mailing in the paperwork. Gathering the data and making yourself aware of all your different options isn't enough to know exactly what to do, however. On the one hand, you can knock yourself out trying to figure out which options are best for you and wondering if you made the best decision. On the other hand, you can work with a financial professional who uses customized software that takes all the variables of your specific situation into account and calculates your best option. You have tens of thousands of different options for filing for your Social Security benefit. If your spouse is a different age than you are, it nearly doubles the amount of options you have. This is far more complicated arithmetic than most people can do on their own. If you want a truly accurate understanding of when and how to file, you need someone who will ask you the right questions about your situation, someone who has access to specialized software that can crunch the numbers. The reality is that you need to work with a professional that can provide you with the sophisticated analysis of your situation that will help you make a truly informed decision.

Important Questions about Your Social Security Benefit:
How can I maximize my lifetime benefit? By knowing when and how to file for Social Security. This usually means waiting until you have at least reached your Full Retirement Age. A professional has the experience and the tools to help determine when and how you can maximize your lifetime benefits.

Who will provide reliable advice for making these decisions? Only a professional has the tools and experience to provide you reliable advice.

Will the Social Security Administration provide me with the advice? The Social Security Administration cannot provide you with advice or strategies for claiming your benefit. They can give you information about your monthly benefit, but that's it. They also don't have the tools to tell you what your specific best option is. They can accurately answer how the system works, but they can't advise you on what decision to make as to how and when to file for benefits.

The Maximization Report that your financial professional will generate represents an invaluable resource for understanding how and when to file for your Social Security benefit. When you get your customized Social Security Maximization Report, you will not only know all the options available to you – but you will understand the financial implications of each choice. In addition to the analysis, you will also get a report that shows *exactly* at what age – including which month and year – you should trigger benefits and how you should apply. It also includes a variety of other time-specific recommendations, such as when to apply for Medicare or take Required Minimum Distributions from your qualified plans. A report means there is no need to wonder, or to try to figure out when to take action – the Social Security Maximization Report lays it all out for you in plain English.

CHAPTER 9 RECAP //

- To get the most out of your Social Security benefit, you need to file at the right time.
- An Investment Advisor can help you determine when you should file for Social Security to get your Maximum Lifetime Benefit.

10

WHEN SOCIAL SECURITY ISN'T ENOUGH

"
MONEY IS A GOOD SERVANT, BUT A
BAD MASTER.

- H.G. Bohn
"

The moment that you stop working and start living off the money that you've set aside for retirement can be referred to as the Retirement Cliff. You've worked and earned money your whole life, but the day that you retire, that income comes to an end. That's the day that you have to have other assets that fill the gap. Social Security will fill in some, but you need to come up with something else. After you have calculated your Social Security benefit and have selected the year and month that will maximize your lifetime benefits, it's time to look at your other retirement assets, incomes and options that will reduce or eliminate the drop-off of the Retirement Cliff. You may have a pension, an IRA or Roth IRA, dividends from stock holdings, money from the sale of real estate, rental property, or other sources of income. What other sources of reliable income do you have?

If your monthly Social Security check and your other supplemental income leaves a shortfall in your *desired* income, how are you going to fix it? This shortfall is called the **Income Gap** and it needs to be filled in order to maintain your lifestyle into retirement. If you have a known income gap that you need to fill, you want to know how to fill that income gap with the fewest dollars possible. You basically want to buy that income gap for the least amount of money possible. You don't want it to cost you too much, because you want to get the most out of your other assets, including planning for your future and planning for your legacy. You do that by maximizing your Social Security benefit, leveraging your additional income and looking at other investment tools that can help generate income for you. Your specific needs, of course, should be analyzed and consulted by a professional.

TAKING A HYBRID APPROACH TO YOUR INCOME NEEDS

You looked at Social Security strategies earlier, discovering you have some control over how and when you file. Those decisions can change the outcome of your benefit in your favor. Once you start drawing that income, it is safer and will provide you with a reliable source of income for the rest of your life. While there are many factors of Social Security that you can control, there are many that you cannot.

For example, you do not have the choice of putting more money into Social Security in order to get more out of it. If you could have the option to contribute more money toward Social Security in order to secure a guaranteed income, it would be a great way to create a Green Money asset that would enhance your retirement. Since that option isn't available, you may seek an investment tool that is similar to Social Security that provides you with a reliable income. It also has the potential to increase the value of your principal investment! This kind of win-win situation exists, and it's called an annuity.

Today, you probably have savings in a variety of assets that you acquired over the years. But you may not have taken time to examine them and assess how they will support your retirement.

It's not about whether the market goes up or down, but when it does. If it goes down at the wrong time for your five or 10 year retirement horizon, you could be in serious danger of losing some of your retirement income.

If you have assets that you would like to structure for retirement income, *an annuity may be the right choice for you.*

Ask yourself the following questions:
- How concerned are you about finding a secure financial vehicle to protect your savings?
- How concerned are you that there may be a better way to structure your savings?

If you are concerned about the best way to fill your income gap, an income annuity investment tool is likely a good option for you. Income annuities have many similar qualities to Social Security that give them the same look and feel as that reliable benefit check you get every month. Most importantly, an income annuity can be an efficient and profitable way to solve your income gap.

HOW ANNUITIES FIT INTO AN OVERALL INCOME PLAN

Annuities are popular and reliable investment tools that allow you to secure income during retirement. In its simplest form, an annuity is a way to invest your money that allows you to structure it for income. Annuities come in a variety of modes. Finding the right one for you will take a conversation with your financial professional. Be sure you fully understand the features, benefits and costs of any annuity you are considering before investing money.

Here is how they can work:

When you put your money into an annuity, you are essentially buying an investment product from an insurance company. It is a contract between you and the insurance company that provides the investment tool. Let's say you have saved $100,000 and need it to generate income to meet your needs above and beyond your Social Security and pension checks. You give the $100,000 to an insurance company, who in turn invests it to generate growth. They usually select investments that have modest returns over long term horizons. In other words, they generally put it somewhere stable and predictable. Most commonly, they will invest it in a combination of bonds and treasuries that are safer and dependable ways to grow money. They use the money from the insurance products they sell to invest, use a portion of the returns to generate profits for themselves, and return a portion to clients in the form of payouts, claims, and structured income options.

One of the most attractive qualities of these types of annuities is something called annual reset. Annual reset is sometimes also referred to as a "ratcheting." Instead of taking on the risk that comes with putting money in a fluctuating market, you can offset that risk onto the insurance company. It works like this: If the market goes down, you don't suffer a loss. Instead, the insurance company absorbs it. But if the market goes up, you share with the insurance company some of the profit made on the gain. The amount of gain you get is called your annuity participation rate. Typically the insurer will cap the amount of gain you can realize at somewhere between 3 and 7 percent. If the market goes up 10 percent, you would realize a portion of that gain (whatever percentage you are capped at). This means you to never lose money on your investment, while always gaining a portion of the upswings. The measurement period of your annuity can be calculated monthly, weekly and even daily, but most annuities are measured annually. The level of the index when you buy and the index level one year later will determine the amount of loss or gain. You and the insurance company are betting that the market will generally go up over time.

INCOME RIDER

When you use that $100,000 to buy a contract with an insurance company in the form of an annuity, you are pegging your money on an index. It could be the S&P 500, the Dow Jones Industrial Average or any number of indexes. To generate income from the annuity, you select something called an income rider. An income rider is a subset of an indexed annuity. Essentially, it is the amount of money from which the insurance company will pay you an income while you have your money in their annuity. Your income rider is a larger number than what your investment is actually worth, and if you select the income rider, it will increase in value over time, providing you with more income. As the insurance company holds your money and invests it, they generate a return on it that they use to pay you a regular monthly income based on a higher number. The insurance company has to outperform the amount that they pay you in order to make a profit.

Remember, insurance companies make long-term investments that provide them with predictable flows of money. They like to stabilize the amount of money that goes in and out of their doors instead of paying and receiving large unpredictable chunks at once. When you opt for an income rider, an insurance company can reliably predict how much money they will pay out to you over a set period of time. It's predictable, and they like that. They can base their business on those predictable numbers.

In order to encourage investors to leave their money in their annuity contracts, insurance companies create surrender periods that protect their investments. If you remove your money from the annuity contract during the surrender period, you will pay a penalty and will not be able to receive your entire investment amount back. A typical surrender period is 10 years. If after three years you decide that you want your $100,000 back, the insurance company has that money tied up in bonds and other investments with the understanding that they will have it for another seven years. Because they will take a hit on removing the money from their investments prematurely, you will have to pay a surrender charge that makes up for their loss. During the surrender period, an annuity is not a demand deposit account like a savings or checking account. The higher returns that you are guaranteed from an annuity are dependent on the timeframe you selected. The longer an insurance company can hold your money, the easier it is for them to guarantee a predictable return on it.

If you leave your money in the annuity contract, you get a reliable monthly income no matter what happens in the market. Once the surrender period has expired, you can remove your money whenever you want. Your money becomes liquid again because the insurance company has used it in an investment that fit the timeline of your surrender period. For many people, this is an attractive trade off that can provide a creative solution for filling their income gap.

When is an annuity with an income rider right for you? A good financial professional can help you make that determination by taking the time to listen closely to your situation and understanding what your needs are as you enter retirement. Every salesperson has a bag full of brochures and PowerPoint presentations, but they need to know exactly what the financial concerns of their individual clients are in order to help them make the most informed and beneficial decision. Some people need income today, others need it in five or 10 years. Others may have their income needs met but are planning to move closer to their children and will need to buy a house in 10 years. Or, if you want income in 15 years, you might want to choose a different investment product for 10 years, and then switch to an annuity with an income rider during the last five years of your timeline. Everyone's situation is different and everyone's needs are different. People who are interested in annuities, however, usually need to make decisions that affect their income needs, whether it is filling their income gap, or providing for income down the road.

What happens if you place on a shorter timeframe those assets from which you need to draw an income? Something called single premium immediate annuities may be for you:

SINGLE PREMIUM IMMEDIATE ANNUITIES (SPIA)

A single premium immediate annuity is simply a contract between you and an insurance company. SPIAs are structured so that you pay a lump sum of money (a single premium) to an insurance company, and they give you a guaranteed income over an agreed upon time period. That time period could be five years, or it could be for the remainder of your lifetime. Guarantees from insurance companies are based on the claims-paying ability of the issuing insurance company.

SPIAs provide investors with a stream of reliable income when they can't afford to take the risk of losing money in a fluctuating market. While there is general faith that the market always trends up, at least in the long-term, if you are focusing on income over a shorter period of time, you may not be able to take a big hit in the market. Beyond normal market volatility, interest rates also come with an inherent level of uncertainty, making it hard to create a dependable income on your own. SPIAs reduce risk for you by giving you regular monthly, quarterly or yearly payments that can begin the moment you buy the contract. Your financial professional can walk you through a series of different payment options to help you select the one that most closely fits your needs.

Additional Annuity Information:
Some contracts will allow you to draw income from the high water mark that the market reaches each year. The income rider will then begin calculating its value from the high water mark.

Variable annuities, however, can lose money with market fluctuations. As their name suggests, they vary with the market. These annuities do not take advantage of annual reset when the market goes down. The income rider will stay the same, but the value of your actual contract may fall. If you surrender the annuity, the insurance company will pay you the market value of the asset, regardless of whether it matches, exceeds or falls short of the value at which you bought the contract. If its value has dropped significantly, you may be better off taking the income rider without surrendering your contract.

Income annuities are investment tools that look and feel a bit like Social Security. Every year you allow the money to grow with the market, and it will "roll up" by a specific amount, paying out a specific percent to you as income each year.

Annuities can work very well to create income, and a financial professional can help you find the one that best matches your income need, and can also structure it to work perfectly for you.

Managing Risk Within Your Annuity:

> **Just like any investment strategy, the amount of risk needs to fit the comfort level of the investor.**

Annuities are no exception. Without going into too much detail, here are some additional ways to manage risk with annuity options:

If you want to structure an annuity investment for growth over a long period of time, you can select a variable annuity. The value of your principal investment follows the market and can lose or gain value with the market. This type of annuity can also have an income rider, but it is really more useful as an accumulation tool that bets on an improving market. A 40-year-old couple, for example, will probably want to structure more for growth and take on more risk than someone in their 70s. The 40-year-old couple may select a variable annuity with an income rider that kicks in when they plan to retire. If it rises with the market or outperforms it, the value of their investment has grown. If the market loses ground over the duration of the contract or their annuity underperforms, they can still rely on the income rider.

If you are 68 years old and you have more immediate income needs that you need to come up with above and beyond your Social Security, you need a low risk, reliable source of income. If you choose an annuity option, you are looking for something that will pay out an income right away over a relatively short timeframe. You probably want to opt for a SPIA that pays you immediately and spans a five year period, as well as an additional annuity that begins paying you in five years, and another longer term annuity that begins paying you in 10 years. Bear in mind that each annuity contract has its own costs and fees. Review these with your financial professional before you determine the best products and strategies for your situation.

The following example shows just how helpful an indexed annuity option can be for a retiree:

> » *Richard and Cynthia are 62 years old and have decided to run the numbers to see what their retirement is going to look like. They know they currently need $6,000 per month to pay their bills and maintain their current lifestyle. They have also done their Social Security homework and have determined that, between the two of them, they will receive $4,200 per month in benefits. They also receive $350 per month in rent from a tenant who lives in a small apartment in their backyard. Between their Social Security and the monthly rent income, they will be short $1,450 per month.*
>
> *They do have an additional asset, however. They have been contributing for years to an IRA that has reached a value of $350,000. They realize that they have to figure out how to turn the $350,000 in their IRA into $1,450 per month for the rest of their life. At first glance, it may seem like they will have plenty of money. With some quick calculations, they find they have 240 months, or nearly 20 years, of monthly income before they exhaust the account. When you consider income tax, the potential for higher taxes in the future, and market fluctuations (because many IRAs are invested in the market), the amount in the IRA seems to have a little less clout. Every dollar Richard and Cynthia take out of the IRA is subject to income tax, and if they leave the remainder in the IRA, they run the risk of losing money in a volatile market. Once they retire and stop getting a paycheck every two weeks, they also stop contributing to their IRA. And when they aren't supplementing its growth with their own money, they are entirely dependent on market growth. That's a scary prospect. They could also withdraw the money from the IRA and put it in a savings account or CD, but removing all the money at once*

will put them in a tax bracket that will claim a huge portion of the value of the IRA. A seemingly straightforward asset has now become a complicated equation. Richard and Cynthia didn't know what to do, so they met with their financial professional.

Their financial professional suggested that they use the money to purchase an indexed annuity with an income rider. They selected an annuity that was designed for their specific situation. They took the lump sum from their IRA, placed it in an indexed annuity taking advantage of annual reset so they never lost the value of their investment. In return, they were guaranteed the $1,450 of income per month that they needed to meet their retirement goals. The simplicity of the contract allowed them to do an analysis with their professional just once to understand the product. They basically put their money in an investment crockpot where they didn't have to look at it or manage it. They just needed to let it simmer. In fact, their professional was able to find an annuity for them that allowed them their $1,450 monthly payment with a lump sum of $249,455, leaving them more than $100,000 to reinvest somewhere else. Keep in mind that annuities are tax deferred, meaning you will pay tax on the income you receive from an annuity in the year you receive it.

» Brenda is 60 years old and is wondering how she can use her assets to provide her with a retirement income. She has a $5,000 per month income need. If she starts withdrawing her Social Security benefit in six years at age 66, it will provide her with $2,200 per month. She also has a pension that kicks in at age 70 that will give her another $1,320 per month.

That leaves an income gap of $2,800 from ages 66 to 69, and then an income gap of $1,480 at age 70 and beyond. If Brenda uses only Green Money to solve her income need, she *will need to deposit $918,360 at 2 percent interest to meet her monthly goal for her lifetime. If she opts to use Red Money and withdraws the amount she needs each month from the market, let's say the S&P 500, she will run out of cash in 10 years if she invested between the years of 2000 and 2012. Suffering a market downturn like that during the period for which she is relying on it for retirement income will change her life, and not for the better.*

Working with a financial professional to find a better way, Brenda found that she could take a hybrid approach to fill her income gap. Her professional recommended two different income vehicles: one that allowed her to deposit just $190,161 with a 2 percent return, and one that was a $146,000 income annuity. These tools filled her income gap with $336,161, requiring her to spend $582,000 less money to accomplish her goal! Working with a professional to find the right tools for her retirement needs saved Brenda over half a million dollars.

CREATING AN INCOME PLAN

Creating an income plan before you retire allows you to satisfy your need for lifetime income and ensures that your lifestyle can last as long as you do.

> **You also want to create a plan that operates in the most efficient way possible.**

Doing so will give more security to your Need Later Money and will potentially allow you to build your legacy down the road.

Here is a basic roadmap of what we have covered so far:

- Review your income needs and look specifically at the shortfall you may have during each year of your retirement based on your Social Security income, and income from any other assets you have.

- Ask yourself where you are in your distribution phase. Is retirement one year away? 10 years away? Last year?
- Determine how much money you need and how you need to structure your existing assets to provide for that need.
- If you have an asset from which you need to generate income, consider options offered by purchasing an income rider on an annuity.

» *Nancy wants to retire at age 68. However, after her Social Security benefit, she will need nearly $375,000 in assets to generate a modest $40,000 of income per year. Amazingly, most people don't look ahead to think that at 68 years old, they will need $375,000 to have a basic lifestyle that pays out around $40,000 with Social Security benefits.*

ACCUMULATION

Understanding your Social Security benefit, filling the income gap and making an overall plan that meets your retirement income needs is no small task. Once you have worked with a financial professional to structure your income needs, it's time to take a look at the future. With your immediate income needs met, you have the opportunity to take your additional assets and leverage them for profit to supplement your income in the future, to prepare for anticipated health care costs or to contribute to your legacy. Stable income also means that you should have the staying power to stick with your investment portfolio through the ups and downs in the market.

MATH OF REBOUNDS

A fickle market can raise the eyebrows of even the most veteran investor. Taking a hit in the market hurts no matter how stable your income. Part of the pain comes from knowing that when you take a step back in the market, it requires an even larger step forward to return to where you were. As the market goes up and down, those larger gains you need to realize to get back to zero start to look even more daunting.

HOW REAL PEOPLE MAKE INVESTMENT DECISIONS

It can be challenging to watch the stock market's erratic changes every month, week or even every day. When you have your money riding on it, the ride can feel pretty bumpy. When you are managing your money by yourself, emotions inevitably enter into the mix. The Dow Jones Industrial Average and the S&P 500 represent more to you than market fluctuations. They represent a portion of your retirement. It's hard not to be emotional about it.

Everyone knows you should buy low and sell high. But this is what is more likely to happen:

The market takes a downturn, similar to the 2008 crash, and investors see as much as a 30 percent loss in their stock holdings. It's hard to watch, and it's harder to bear the pain of losing that much money. The math of rebounds means that they will need to rely on even larger gains just to get back to where things were before the downturn. They sell. But eventually, and inevitably, the market begins to rise again. Maybe slowly, maybe with some moderate growth, but by the time the average investor notices an upward trend and wants to buy in again, they have already missed a great deal of the gains.

CHAPTER 10 RECAP //

- Having an income plan will help you get a picture of what your retirement is really going to look like.
- You have *Need Now Money* needs and *Need Later Money* needs. Creating an income plan is the first step toward providing for both of these needs.
- Maximizing your Social Security benefit depends on *when* and *how* you file.
- You'll need to examine your specific situation to find the best option for you.
- It's not impossible for you to calculate when the opportune time would be to trigger your Social Security income. In fact, with the tools and advice of a financial professional, it's quite easy.
- Integrating your Social Security options with the rest of your income plan will give you an idea of how much more money you need.
- Every dollar your Social Security income increases is less money you'll have to spend from your nest egg to supplement your income.
- After Social Security and your additional income is accounted for, the amount that's left to meet your needs is called the *Income Gap*.
- It is important to find ways to leverage your retirement assets to satisfy your need for lifetime income.
- It has been ages since many stocks returned meaningful dividends, so it isn't advisable to rely on them for reliable income. However, without stocks, your retirement plan will likely lose ground to inflation.
- It might be very attractive to have another asset, such as an annuity, that is designed to give you lifetime income. That income can go up in value as you wait to trigger a monthly check.

- If you think maximizing your Social Security isn't enough and you need the rest of your assets to be optimized to fill the income gap, an annuity may be a good option for you.
- Creating a retirement plan that focuses only on providing income will eventually have you cutting into your principle, drying it up in time and leaving you sucking up the last remaining drops.
- Although an annuity is an income-producing asset that does not subject your income to market risk, it still has the opportunity to grow.
- Be sure you understand the features, benefits, costs and fees associated with any annuity product before you invest.

PART THREE:
FOCUS ON THE
FINISH LINE

Let's finish the story of our client Margaret. To refresh your memory, Margaret, a part-time nurse, came to visit with us after her mother passed away. A dedicated saver just like her parents, Margaret had amassed some savings, even after she went part-time to care for her ailing mother, but she feared she hadn't been able to save enough and would be living on a tight fixed income in her retired days. Margaret's parents taught her the value of saving, but, as kids of the Depression, they weren't keen on talking about what money they had, if any. And so, when Margaret came to see us, she had no idea what was awaiting her.

We were delighted to give Margaret the good news. Margaret's mom had actually been a very active financial planner. She had worked with five different financial professionals, had saved a significant amount and established a healthy annuity. The farm was also a significant asset. Margaret and her sister would be able to retire, and comfortably, when they were ready.

Unfortunately, we had some bad news too. One of Margaret's mother's advisors had failed to list beneficiaries on her largest asset, a $250,000 IRA. With no beneficiary, the IRA goes to the estate and must go through lengthy probate proceedings. Plus, the income becomes taxable immediately, which meant significant tax increases for Margaret and her sister that year. Had she, as the executor, or her mother come to us just a few months earlier, we would have double checked for crucial mistakes like that one. As it was, we could do nothing to help.

Even with that painful error, Margaret's financial future was so much brighter than she'd imagined. When all the numbers were laid out before her, she grew very quiet for a moment and then began to cry. We were worried at first, and grabbed for the tissue we keep in every conference room for just these occasions.

"Are you alright, Margaret?"

She nodded and, finally, her face broke into a huge smile. "I'm so much better than alright. Until now, I wasn't sure if I'd ever get to retire at all."

So here we are. You're closing in on your actual retirement, the day you will enter a whole new era of freedom and adventure. And we want it to be everything you imagine. Actually we want it to be better. So, remember Margaret. Do all of your planning, and even if your work with a professional, always get another professional to double check your paperwork. For your retired years and after, you want to be sure that everything goes exactly as planned. Whether your dream is to buy a vacation home in Paris or send your grandkids to college, it's worth a second opinion, don't you think?

In this phase, you're making a change in mindset. You're transitioning from amassing new savings to protecting everything you've collected. Your financial team will be a huge asset as you make this change.

11
THE MARKET AND
YOUR MONEY

Pamela has worked for Acme Paper Company for 34 years. During her time there, she has acquired bonuses and pay raises that often included shares of stock in the company. She has also dedicated part of her paycheck every month to a 401(k) that bought Acme stock. By the time she retires, Pamela has $250,000 worth of Acme stock.

Although she contributed to her 401(k) account every month, Pamela hasn't cultivated any other assets that could generate income for her during retirement. Pamela also retires early at age 62 because of her failing health. The commute to work every day was becoming difficult in her weakened condition and she wanted to enjoy the rest of her life in retirement instead of working at Acme.

Because she retires early, Pamela fails to maximize her Social Security benefit. While she lives a modest lifestyle, her income needs will still be $3,500 per month. Pamela's monthly Social Security check *will only cover $1,900, leaving her with a $1,600 income gap. To supplement her Social Security check, Pamela sells $1,600 of her Acme stock each month to meet her income needs. A $250,000 401(k) is nothing to sneeze at, but reducing its value by $1,600 every month will barely last Pamela 10 years. And that's if the market stays neutral or grows modestly. If the market takes a downturn, the money that Pamela relied on to fill her income gap will rapidly diminish. Even if the market starts going up in a couple of years, it will take much larger gains for her to recover the value that she lost.*

Unhappily for Pamela, she retired in 2007, just before the major market downturn that lasted for several years. She lost more than 20 percent of the value of her stock. Because Pamela needed to sell her stock to meet her basic income needs, the market price of the stock was secondary to her need for the money. When she needed money, she was forced to sell however many shares she needed to fill her income gap that month. And if she has a financial crisis, involving her need for medical care, for example, she will be forced to sell stock even if the market is low and her shares are nearly worthless.

Pamela realizes that she could have relied on an investment structured to deliver her a regular income while protecting the value of her investment. She could have kept her $250,000 from diminishing while enjoying her lifestyle into retirement regardless of the volatility of the market. Ideally, Pamela would have restructured her 401(k) to reflect the level of risk that she was able to take. In her case, she would have had most of her money in Green Money assets, allowing her to rely on the value of her assets when she needed them.

In 2013, DALBAR, the well-respected financial services market research firm, released their annual "Quantitative Analysis of Investment Behavior" report (QAIB). The report studied the impact of market volatility on individual investors: people like *Pamela*, or anyone who was managing (or mismanaging) their own investments in the stock market.

According to the study, volatility not only caused investors to make decisions based on their emotions, those decisions also harmed their investments and prevented them from realizing potential gains. So why do people meddle so much with their investments when the market is fluctuating? Part of the reason is that many people have financial obligations that they don't have control over. Significant expenses like house payments, the unexpected cost of replacing a broken-down car, and medical bills can put people in a position where they need money. If they need to sell investments to come up with that money, they don't have the luxury of selling when they *want* to. They must sell when they *need* to.

DALBAR's "Quantitative Analysis of Investor Behavior" has been used to measure the effects of investors' buying, selling and mutual fund switching decisions since 1994. The QAIB shows time and time again over nearly a 20 year period that the average investor earns less, and in many cases, significantly less than the performance of mutual funds suggests. QAIB's goal is to improve independent investor performance and to help financial professionals provide helpful advice and investment strategies that address the concerns and behaviors of the average investor.

An excerpt from the report claims that:

"QAIB offers guidance on how and where investor behaviors can be improved. No matter what the state of the mutual fund industry, boom or bust: Investment results are more dependent on investor behavior than on fund performance. Mutual fund investors who hold on to their investments are more successful than those who time the market.

QAIB uses data from the Investment Company Institute (ICI), Standard & Poor's and Barclays

Capital Index Products to compare mutual fund investor returns to an appropriate set of benchmarks.

There are actually three primary causes for the chronic shortfall for both equity and fixed income investors:

Capital not available to invest. This accounts for 25 percent to 35 percent of the shortfall.

Capital needed for other purposes. This accounts for 35 percent to 45 percent of the shortfall.

Psychological factors. These account for 45 percent to 55 percent of the shortfall."

The key findings of Dalbar's QAIB report provide compelling statistics about how individual investment strategies produced negative outcomes for the majority of investors:

- Psychological factors account for 45 percent to 55 percent of the chronic investment return shortfall for both equity and fixed income investors.
- Asset allocation is designed to handle the investment decision-making for the investor, which can materially reduce the shortfall due to psychological factors.
- Successful asset allocation investing requires investors to act on two critical imperatives:
- Balance capital preservation and appreciation so that they are aligned with the investor's objective.
- Select a qualified allocator.
- The best way for an investor to determine their risk tolerance is to utilize a risk tolerance assessment. However, these assessments must be accessible and usable.
- Evaluating allocator quality requires analysis of the allocator's underlying investments, decision making process and whether or not past efforts have produced successful outcomes.
- Choosing a top allocator makes a significant difference in the investment results one will achieve.

- Mutual fund retention rates suggest that the average investor has not remained invested for long enough periods to derive the potential benefits of the investment markets.
- Retention rates for asset allocation funds exceed those of equity and fixed income funds by over a year.
- Investors' ability to correctly time the market is highly dependent on the direction of the market. Investors generally guess right more often in up markets. However, in 2012 investors guessed right only 42 percent of the time during a bull market.
- Analysis of investor fund flows compared to market performance further supports the argument that investors are unsuccessful at timing the market. Market upswings rarely coincide with mutual fund inflows while market downturns do not coincide with mutual fund outflows.
- Average equity mutual fund investors gained 15.56 percent compared to a gain of 15.98 percent that just holding the S&P 500 produced.
- The shortfall in the long-term annualized return of the average mutual fund equity investor and the S&P 500 continued to decrease in 2012.
- The fixed-income investor experienced a return of 4.68 percent compared to an advance of 4.21 percent on the Barclays Aggregate Bond Index.
- The average fixed income investor has failed to keep up with inflation in nine out of the last 14 years.*

It doesn't take a financial services market research report to tell you that market volatility is out of your control. The report does prove, however, that before you experience market volatility, you should have an investment plan, and when the market is fluctuating, you

---

*2013 QAIB, Dalbar, March 2013

should stand by your investment plan. You should also review and discuss your investment plan with your financial professional on a regular basis, ensuring he/she is aware of any changes in your goals, financial circumstances, your health or your risk tolerance.

> **When the economy is under stress and the markets are volatile, investors can feel vulnerable.**

That vulnerability causes people to tinker with their portfolios in an attempt to outsmart the market. Financial professionals, however, don't try to time the market for their clients. They try to tap into the gains that can be realized by committing to long-term investment strategies.

12
PAYING TAXES AS A RETIREE

> THE PROBLEM IS NOT THAT PEOPLE ARE TAXED TOO LITTLE; THE PROBLEM IS THAT GOVERNMENT SPENDS TOO MUCH.
>
> *- Ronald Reagan*

Another of our clients, Dennis, offers a great example of how important it is to understand the impact of taxes on how you take your money out. Dennis is wrapping up his career with Border Protection, and we've been working with him for several years, getting everything arranged for his retirement. As we made the final preparations for his retirement, we asked him to send us a list of his monthly expenses, *including debt he's paying off. There's about $35,000 in debt he'll need to pay off, his credit card and house, and he already had a plan: pull enough money out of retirement to pay those off immediately.*

Paying off debt is a great plan, but when you're pulling the money out of retirement to do so, there are special considerations. He'll have to pay taxes on that withdrawal, which means he'd actually have to take out closer to $60,000. What's more, that huge withdrawal would move him up from the 15 percent tax bracket into the 25-28 percent bracket, which in turn means he'd actually need an even LARGER withdrawal to pay the higher taxes.

We had another idea: take the money out in installments over several years, still paying off big chunks of debt at a time, but not everything at once. In the end, he'd still pay off his debt and save nearly $9,000 in taxes.

Taxes play a starring role in the theater of retirement planning. Everyone is familiar with taxes (you've been paying them your entire working life), but not everyone is familiar with how to make tax planning a part of their retirement strategy.

Taxes are taxes, right? You'll pay them before retirement and you'll pay them during retirement. What's the difference? The truth is that a planful approach to taxes can help you save money, protect your assets and ensure that your legacy remains intact.

How can a tax form do all that? The answer lies in planning. **Tax planning** and **tax reporting** are two very different things. Most people only *report* their taxes. March rolls around, people pull out their 1040s or use TurboTax to enter their income and taxable assets, and ship it off to Uncle Sam at the IRS. If you use a CPA to report your taxes, you are essentially paying them to record history. You have the option of being proactive with your taxes and to plan for your future by making smart, informed decisions about how taxes affect your overall financial plan. Working with a financial professional who, along with a CPA, makes recommendations about your finances to you, will keep you looking forward instead of in the rearview mirror as you enter retirement.

TAXES AND RETIREMENT

When you retire, you move from the earning and accumulation phase of your life into the asset distribution phase of your life. For most people, that means relying on Social Security, a 401(k), an IRA, or a TSP. Wherever you have put your Green Money for retirement, you are going to start relying on it to provide you with the income that once came as a paycheck. Most of these distributions will be considered income by the IRS and will be taxed as such. There are exceptions to that (not all of your Social Security income is taxed, and income from Roth IRAs is not taxed), but for the most part, your distributions will be subject to income taxes.

Regarding assets that you have in an IRA, a 401(k) plan that uses an IRA, or a TSP, when you reach 70 ½ years of age, you will be required to draw a certain amount of money from your IRA as income each year. That amount depends on your age and the balance in your IRA. The amount that you are required to withdraw as income is called a Required Minimum Distribution (RMD). Why are you required to withdraw money from your own account? Chances are the money in that account has grown over time, and the government wants to collect taxes on that growth. If you have a large balance in an IRA, there's a chance your RMD could increase your income significantly enough to put you into a higher tax bracket, subjecting you to a higher tax rate.

Here's where tax planning can really begin to work strongly in your favor. In the distribution phase of your life, you have a predictable income based on your RMDs, your Social Security benefit and any other income-generating assets you may have. What really impacts you at this stage is how much of that money you keep in your pocket after taxes. Essentially, ***you will make*** *more money saving on taxes than you will by making more money.* If you can reduce your tax burden by 30, 20 or even 10 percent, you earn yourself that much more money by not paying it in taxes.

How do you save money on taxes? By having a plan. In this instance, a financial professional can work with the CPAs at their firm to create a **distribution plan** that minimizes your taxes and maximizes your annual net income.

BUILDING A TAX DIVERSIFIED PORTFOLIO

So far so good: avoid taxes, maximize your net annual income and have a plan for doing it. When people decide to leverage the experience and resources of a financial professional, they may not be thinking of how distribution planning and tax planning will benefit their portfolios. Often more exciting prospects like planning income annuities, investing in the market and structuring investments for growth rule the day. Taxes, however, play a crucial role in retirement planning. Achieving those tax goals requires knowledge of options, foresight and professional guidance.

Finding the path to a good tax plan isn't always a simple task.

Every tax return you file is different from the one before it because things constantly change. Your expenses change. Planned or unplanned purchases occur. Health care costs, medical bills, an inheritance, property purchases, reaching an age where your RMD kicks in or travel, any number of things can affect how much income you report and how many deductions you take each year.

Preparing for the ever-changing landscape of your financial life requires a tax-diversified portfolio that can be leveraged to balance the incomes, expenditures and deductions that affect you each year. A financial professional will work with you to answer questions like these:

- What does your tax landscape look like?
- Do you have a tax-diversified portfolio robust enough to adapt to your needs?
- Do you have a diversity of taxable and non-taxable income planned for your retirement?
- Will you be able to maximize your distributions to take advantage of your deductions when you retire?
- Is your portfolio strong enough and tax-diversified enough to adapt to an ever-changing (and usually increasing) tax code?

» *When Elizabeth returns home after a week in the hospital recovering from a knee replacement, the 67-year-old calls her daughter, sister and brother to let them know she is home and feeling well. She also should have called her CPA. Elizabeth's medical expenses for the procedure, her hospital stay, her medications and the ongoing physical therapy she attended amount to more than $50,000.*

Currently, Americans can deduct medical expenses that are more than 7.5 percent of their Adjusted Gross Income (AGI). Elizabeth's AGI is $60,000 the year of her knee replacement, meaning she is able to deduct $44,000 of her medical bills from her taxes that year. Her AGI dictated that she could deduct more than 80 percent of her medical expenses that year. **Elizabeth didn't know this***.*

Had she been working with a financial professional who regularly asked her about any changes in her life, her spending, or her expenses (expected or unexpected), Elizabeth could have saved thousands of dollars. Elizabeth can also file an amendment to her tax return to recoup the overpayment.

This relatively simple example of how tax planning can save you money is just the tip of the iceberg. No one can be expected to know the entire U.S. tax code. But a professional who is working with a team of CPAs and financial professionals have an advantage over the average taxpayer who must start from square one on their own every year. Have you been taking advantage of all the deductions that are available to you?

PROACTIVE TAX PLANNING

The implications of proactive tax planning are far reaching, and are larger than many people realize. Remember, doing your taxes in January, February, March or April means you are writing a history book. Planning your taxes in October, November or December means that you are writing the story as it happens. You can look at all the factors that are at play and make decisions that will impact your tax return *before* you file it.

Realizing that tax planning is an aspect of financial planning is an important leap to make. When you incorporate tax planning into your financial planning strategy, it becomes part of the way you maximize your financial potential. Paying less in taxes means you keep more of your money. Simply put, the more money you keep, the more of it you can leverage as an asset. This kind of planning can affect you at any stage of your life. If you are 40 years old, are you contributing the maximum amount to your 401(k) plan or TSP? Are you contributing to a Roth IRA? Are you finding ways to structure the savings you are dedicating to your children's education? Do you have life insurance? Taxes and tax planning affects all of these investment tools. Having a relationship with a professional who works with a CPA can help you build a truly comprehensive financial plan that not only works with your investments, but also shapes your assets to find the most efficient ways to prepare for tax time. There may be years that you could benefit from higher distributions because of the tax bracket that you are in, or there could be years you would benefit from taking less. There may be years when you have a lot of deductions and years you have relatively few. **Adapting your distributions to work in concert with your available deductions** is at the heart of smart tax planning. Professional guidance can bring you to the next level of income distribution, allowing you to remain flexible enough to maximize your tax efficiency. And remember, saving money on taxes makes you more money than making money does.

What you have on paper is important: your assets, savings, investments, which are financial expression of your work and time. It's just as important to know how to get it off the paper in a way that keeps most of it in your pocket. Almost anything that involves financial planning also involves taxes. Annuities, investments, IRAs, 401(k)s, 403(b), TSPs and many other investment options will have tax implications. Life also has a way of throwing curveballs. Illness, expensive car repair or replacement, or *any event that has a financial impact on your life will likely have a corresponding tax implication* around which you should adapt your financial plan. Tax planning does just that.

One dollar can end up being less than 25 cents to your heirs.

> » When Luke's father passed away, he discovered that he was the beneficiary of his father's $500,000 IRA. Luke has a wife and a family of four children, and he knew that his father had intended for a large portion of the IRA to go toward funding their college educations.
>
> After Luke's father's estate is distributed, Peter, who is 50 years old and whose two oldest sons are entering college, liquidates the IRA. By doing so, his taxable income for that year puts him in a 39.6 percent tax bracket, immediately reducing the value of the asset to $302,000. An additional 3.8 percent

surtax on net investment income further diminishes the funds to $283,000. Liquidating the IRA in effect subjects much of Luke's regular income to the surtax, as well. At this point, Luke will be taxed at 43.4 percent.

Luke's state taxes are an additional 9 percent. Moreover, estate taxes on Luke's father's assets claim another 22 percent. By the time the IRS is through, Luke's income from the IRA will be taxed at 75 percent, leaving him with $125,000 of the original $500,000. While it would help contribute to the education of his children, it wouldn't come anywhere near completely paying for it, something the $500,000 could have easily done.

As the above example makes clear, leaving an asset to your beneficiaries can be more complicated than it may seem. In the case of a traditional IRA, after federal, estate and state taxes, the asset could literally diminish to as little as 25 percent of its value.

How does working with a professional help you make smarter tax decisions with your own finances? Any financial professional worth their salt will be working with a firm that has a team of trained tax professionals, including CPAs, who have an intimate knowledge of the tax code and how to adapt a financial plan to it.

Here's another example of how taxes have major implications on asset management:

» Greg and Rhonda, a 62-year-old couple, begin working with a financial professional in October. After structuring their assets to reflect their risk tolerance and creating assets that would provide them Green Money income during retirement, they feel good about their situation. They make decisions that allow them to maximize their Social Security benefits, they have plenty of options for filling their income gap, and have begun a safe yet ambitious Yellow Money strat-

egy with their professional. When their professional asks them about their tax plan, they tell him their CPA handled their taxes every year, and did a great job. Their professional says, "I don't mean who does your taxes, I mean, who does your tax planning?" Greg and Rhonda aren't sure how to respond.

Their professional brings Greg and Rhonda's financial plan to the firm's CPA and has her run a tax projection for them. A week later their professional calls them with a tax plan for the year that will save them more than $3,000 on their tax return. The couple is shocked. A simple piece of advice from the CPA based on the numbers revealed that if they paid their estimated taxes before the end of the year, they would be able to itemize it as a deduction, allowing them to save thousands of dollars.

This solution won't work for everyone, and it may not work for Greg and Rhonda every year. That's not the point. By being proactive with their approach to taxes and using the resources made available by their financial professional, they were able to create a tax plan that saved them money.

YELLOW MONEY AND TAXES

There are also tax implications for the money that you have managed professionally. People with portions of their investment portfolio that are actively traded can particularly benefit from having a proactive tax strategy. Without going into too much detail, for tax purposes there are two kinds of investment money: qualified and non-qualified. Different investment strategies can have different effects on how you are taxed on your investments and the growth of your investments. Some are more beneficial for one kind of investment strategy over another. Determining how to plan for the taxation of non-qualified and qualified investments is fodder for holiday party discussions at accounting firms. While it may not be a stimulating topic for the average investor, you don't have to understand exactly how it works in order to benefit from it.

While there are many differences between qualified and non-qualified investments, the main difference is this: qualified plans are designed to give investors tax benefits by deferring taxation of their growth until they are withdrawn. Non-qualified investments are not eligible for these deferral benefits. As such, non-qualified investments are taxed whenever income is realized from them in the form of growth.

Actively and non-actively traded investments provide a simple example of how to position your investments for the best tax advantage. In an actively traded and managed portfolio, there is a high amount of buying and selling of stocks, bonds, funds, ETFs, etc. If that active portfolio of non-qualified investments does well and makes a 20 percent return one year and you are in the 39.6 percent tax bracket, your net gain from that portfolio is only about 12 percent (39.6 percent tax of the 20 percent gain is roughly 8 percent.) In a passive trading strategy, you can use a qualified investment tool, such as an IRA, to achieve 13, 14 or 15 percent growth (much lower than the actively traded portfolio), but still realize a higher net return because the growth of the qualified investment is not taxed until it is withdrawn.

Does this mean that you have to always rely on a buy and hold strategy in qualified investment tools? Not necessarily. The question is, if you have qualified and non-qualified investments, where do you want to position your actively traded and managed assets? Incorporating a planful approach to positioning your investments for more beneficial taxation can be done many ways, but let's consider one example. Keeping your actively managed investment strategies inside an IRA or some other qualified plan could allow you to realize the higher gains of those investments without paying tax on their growth every year. Your more passively managed funds could then be kept in taxable, non-qualified vehicles and methods, and because you aren't realizing income from them on an annual basis by frequently trading them, they grow sheltered from taxation.

If you are interested in taking advantage of tax strategies that maximize your net income, you need the attentive strategies, experience and knowledge of a professional who can give you options that position you for profit. At the end of the day, what's important to you as the consumer is how much you keep, your after-tax take home.

ESTATE TAXES

The government doesn't just tax your income from investments while you're alive. They will also dip into your legacy.

While estate taxes aren't as hot of a topic as they were a few years ago, they are still an issue of concern for many people with assets. While taxes may not apply on estates that are less than $5 million, certain states have estate taxes with much lower exclusion ratios. Some are as low as $600,000. Many people may have to pay a state estate tax. One strategy for avoiding those types of taxes is to move assets outside of your estate. That can include gifting them to family or friends, or putting them into an irrevocable trust. Life insurance is another option for protecting your legacy.

THE FUTURE OF U.S. TAXATION

Tax legislation over the course of American history has left one very resounding message: taxes go up. Sadly, we hear this same threat so often that it has begun to sound like the boy who cried wolf. The reason behind this lies in the fact that tax hikes usually do not take effect until two or three years after their introduction and subsequently get piecemeal implementation. The result of this prolonged implementation period can be equated to death by a thousand paper cuts.

DEBT CEILING – CAUSE AND EFFECTS

The raising of the debt ceiling raised more than just the ability for our government to go further into debt. It also raised concerns and fears about the future of our economy. We are now seeing major swings in the markets with investors showing serious concerns over the future of investment valuations and their personal wealth. Unfortunately, the reasoning behind all of this uncertainty is preceded by the inability to see the full implications of what is in store. We rarely talk about the fact that the discussions on raising the debt ceiling were coupled to discussions on major tax reforms needed to correct the problems underlining the debt ceiling increase itself.

Increasing the debt ceiling was needed because the government maxed out its credit card, so to speak, which it has been living off of for quite some time. It is really not much different than what we have been seeing from the general public for the past few decades. Unfortunately, most of us do not have the ability to get a credit limit increase on our credit cards once we reach the maximum limit unless we can show the ability to pay this balance back. The only way to pay this credit card back is by spending less and making more money.

This is exactly where the federal government is today. They have been given a higher credit limit, but they still must find a way to decrease their spending while making more money. The only way the government makes money is by collecting taxes. Unfortunately, at the current moment, the government is collecting approximately $120 billion less per month than it currently spends. Discussions for major tax reform have accompanied the discussions for the increased debt ceiling.

DEBT AND EARNINGS

Let us take a closer look at where we are today. The U.S. national debt is increasing at an alarming rate, rising to levels never seen before and threatening serious harm to the economy. Through the end of 2010, the national debt has risen to $13.6 trillion, averaging an 11.4 percent increase annually over the past five years and a 9.2 percent increase annually over the past 10 years. To put this into perspective, the national gross domestic product (GDP) has increased to $14.5 trillion during the same period, averaging a 2.9 percent annual increase over the past five years and a 3.9 percent increase over the past 10 years. At the end of 2010, the national debt level was 93 percent of the GDP. Economists believe that a sustainable economy exists at a maximum level of approximately 80 percent. As of December 20, 2013, the U.S. national debt is 107.69 percent of GDP with the debt at $17.252 trillion and the GDP at $16.020 trillion.*

The significance of these two numbers lies within the contrast. The national debt is the amount that needs to be repaid. This is the credit card balance. Gross domestic product on the other hand is less known and represents the market value of all final goods and services produced within a country during a given period. Essentially, GDP represents the gross taxable income available to the government. If debts are increasing at a greater rate than the gross income available for taxation, then the only way to make up the difference is by increasing the rate at which the gross income is taxed.

The most recent presidential budget shows a continuing trend in the disparity between growth in the national debt and GDP over the next two decades. Although the increasing disparity is a real concern and shows that, at least in the short run, the federal deficit will not be addressed to counteract the potential crisis ahead, it is the revenue collection that tells the disconcerting story. Over the past 40 years the average collection of GDP has

*http://www.usdebtclock.org/ 12/20/13

been approximately 17.6 percent and currently collections are at approximately 14.4 percent of GDP.

As the presidential budget reveals, the projected revenues are estimated to be 20 percent by the end of the next decade. That is a 38.8 percent increase from the current tax levels. To put this into perspective, if you are currently in the top tax bracket of 35 percent and this bracket increases by the proposed collection increase, your tax rate will be approximately 48.5 percent. Keep in mind that even at this rate the deficit is projected to increase.

2013 – THE END OF AN ERA?

From a historical point of view, taxes are extremely low. The last time the U.S. national debt was at the same percentage level of GDP as today was at the end of World War II and several years following. The maximum tax rate averaged 90 percent from 1944 through 1963. Compare that to the maximum rate of 35 percent today and it becomes very clear that there is a disparity of extreme proportion.

Taxes during this historical period were at extreme levels for nearly 20 years, during and following this current level of debt-to-GDP. A significant point to note about the difference between that time and today is the economic activity. The period of 1944 through 1963 was in the heart of both the industrial revolution and the birth of the Baby Boom generation. Today, we are mired in extreme volatility with frequent periods of boom and bust at the same time we are witnessing the beginning of the greatest retirement wave ever experienced within the U.S. economy.

To contrast these two time periods in respect to the recovery period is almost asinine as the external pressures from globalization and domestic unfunded liabilities did not exist or were irrelevant factors during the prior period.

To add insult to injury, U.S. domestic unfunded liabilities are currently estimated somewhere around $61.6 trillion above due to items such as Social Security, Medicare and government pensions. The most concerning part of this pertains to the coming wave of retirement as the Baby Boom generation begins retiring and drawing on the unfunded Social Security for which they currently have entitlement. Over the long run, expenditures related to healthcare programs such as Medicare and Medicaid are projected to grow faster than the economy overall as the population matures.

To put unfunded liabilities into perspective, consider these as off-balance-sheet obligations similar to those of Enron. Although these are not listed as part of the national debt, they must be paid. These liabilities exist outside of the annual budgetary debt discussed. The difference between Enron and the U.S. unfunded liabilities is that if the U.S. government cannot come up with the funds to pay all these liabilities through revenue generation, they will print the money necessary to pay the debt.

WHAT DOES THE SOLUTION LOOK LIKE?

Unfortunately, the general public is in a no-win situation for this solution to the problem. Printing money does not bode well for economic growth. This creates inflationary pressures that devalue the U.S. dollar and make everyone less wealthy. Cutting the entitlements that compose this liability leaves millions of people with fewer benefits than they may have come to expect. The only other option, and one that the government knows all too well, is increasing taxes. In fact, according to a Congressional Budget Office paper issued in 2004:

"The term 'unfunded liability' has been used to refer to a gap between the government's projected financial commitment under a particular program and the revenues that are expected to be available to fund that commitment. But no government obligation can be truly considered 'unfunded' because of the U.S. government's sovereign power to tax – which is the ultimate resource to meet its obligations."

A balanced budget will be required at some point and with this will come higher taxes. We have uncertainty surrounding tax rates and how high they will go. At that time, extensions put in place in December 2010 on Bush-era tax cuts are set to expire. We are likely to see some tax increases at this point. Whether it is only on the top earners or unilaterally across all income levels is yet to be seen, but an increase of some sort will most certainly occur.

How do you prepare? Why spend so much time reassuring you that taxes will increase? Because you have an opportunity to take action. Now is the time to prepare for what will come and structure countermeasures for the good, the bad and the ugly of each of these legislative nightmares through tax-advantaged retirement planning.

You make more money by saving on taxes than you do by making more money. The simplistic logic of the statement makes sense when you discover it takes $1.50 in earnings to put that same dollar, saved in taxes, back in your pocket.

As simple as it sounds, it is much more difficult to execute. Most people fail to put together a plan as they near retirement, beginning with a simple cash flow budget. If you have not analyzed your proposed income streams and expenses, you could not possibly have taken the time to position these cash flows and other events into a tax-preferred plan.

Most people will state that they have a plan and, thus, do not need any further assistance in this area. The truth in most instances is that people could not show you their plan, and among the few that could, most would not be able to show you how they have executed it. In this regard, they might as well be Richard Nixon stating, "I am not a crook" for as much as they state, "I have a plan." The truth lies in waiting. As we approach or begin retirement, we should look at what cash flows we will have. Do we have a pension? How about Social Security? How much additional cash flow am I going to need to draw from my assets to maintain the lifestyle that I desire?

> **We spend our whole lives saving and accumulating wealth but spend so little time determining how to distribute this accumulation so as to retain it.**

We need to make sure we have the appropriate diversification of taxable versus non-taxable assets to complement our distribution strategy.

THE BENEFITS OF DIVERSIFICATION

Heading into retirement, we should be situated with a diversified tax landscape. The point to spending our whole lives accumulating wealth is not to see the size of the number on paper, but rather to be an exercise in how much we put in our pocket after removing it from the paper. To truly understand tax diversification, we must understand what types of money exist and how each of these will be treated during accumulation and, most importantly, during distribution. The following is a brief summary:

1. Free money
2. Tax-advantaged money
3. Tax-deferred money
4. Taxable money
   a. Ordinary income
   b. Capital gains and qualified dividends

FREE MONEY

> **Free money is the best kind of money regardless of tax treatment because, in the end, you have more money than you would have otherwise.**

Many employers will provide contributions toward employee retirement accounts to offer additional employment benefits and encourage employees to save for their own retirement. With this, employers often will offer a matching contribution in which they contribute up to a certain percentage of an employee's salary (generally three to five percent) toward that employee's retirement account when the employee contributes to their retirement account as well. For example, if an employee earns $50,000 annually and contributes three percent ($1,500) to their retirement account annually, the employer will also contribute three percent ($1,500) to the employee's account. That is $1,500 in free money. Take all you can get! Bear in mind that any employer contribution to a 401(k) will still be subject to taxation when withdrawn.

TAX-ADVANTAGED MONEY

Tax-advantaged money is the next best thing to free money. Although you have to earn tax-advantaged money, you do not have to give part of it away to Uncle Sam. Tax-advantaged money comes in three basic forms that you can utilize during your lifetime; four if prison inspires your future, but we are not going to discuss that option.

One of the most commonly known forms of tax-advantaged money is municipal bonds, which earn and pay interest that could be tax-advantaged on the federal level, or state level, or both. There are several caveats that should be discussed with regard to the notion of tax-advantaged income from municipal bonds. First, you will notice that tax-advantaged has several flavors from the state and federal perspective. This is because states will generally tax the interest earned on a municipal bond unless the bond is offered from an entity located within that state. This severely limits the availability of completely tax-advantaged municipal bonds and constrains underlying risk and liquidity factors. Second, municipal bond interest is added back into the equation for determining your modified adjusted gross income (MAGI) for Social Security. This could push your income above a threshold and subject a portion of your Social Security income to taxation. In effect, if this interest subjects some other income to taxation then this interest is truly being taxed.

Last, municipal bond interest may be excluded from the regular federal tax system, but it is included for determining tax under the alternative minimum tax (AMT) system. In its basic form, the AMT system is a separate tax system that applies if the tax computed under AMT exceeds the tax computed under the regular tax system. The difference between these two computations is the alternative minimum tax.

TAX-ADVANTAGED MONEY: ROTH IRA

Roth accounts are probably the single greatest tax asset that has come from Congress outside of life insurance. They are well known but rarely used. Roth IRAs were first established by the Taxpayer Relief Act of 1997 and named after Senator William Roth, the chief sponsor of the legislation. Roth accounts are simply an account in the form of an individual retirement account or an employer sponsored retirement account that allows for tax-advantaged growth of earnings and, thus, tax-advantaged income.

The main difference between a Roth and a traditional IRA or employer-sponsored plan lies in the timing of the taxation. We are all very familiar with the typical scenario of putting money away for retirement through an employer plan, whereby they deduct money from our paychecks and put it directly into a retirement account. This money is taken out before taxes are calculated, meaning we do not pay tax on those earnings today. A Roth account, on the other hand, takes the money after the taxes have been removed and puts it into the retirement account, so we do pay tax on the money today. The other significant difference between these two is taxation during distribution in later years. Regarding our traditional retirement accounts, when we take the money out later it is added to our ordinary income and is taxed

161

accordingly. Additionally, including this in our income subjects us to the consequences mentioned above for municipal bonds with Social Security taxation, AMT, as well as higher Medicare premiums. A Roth on the other hand is distributed tax-advantaged and does not contribute toward negative impact items such as Social Security taxation, AMT, or Medicare premium increases. It essentially comes back to us without tax and other obligations.

The best way to view the difference between the two accounts is to look at the life of a farmer. A farmer will buy seed, plant it in the ground, grow the crops and harvest it later for sale. Typically, the farmer would only pay tax on the crops that have been harvested and sold. But if you were the farmer, would you rather pay tax on the $5,000 of seed that you plant today or the $50,000 of crops harvested later? The obvious answer is $5,000 of seed today. The truth to the matter is that you are a farmer, except you plant dollars into your retirement account instead of seeds into the earth.

So why doesn't everyone have a Roth retirement account if things are so simple? There are several reasons, but the single greatest reason has been the constraints on contributions. If you earned over certain thresholds (MAGI over $125,000 single and $183,000 joint for 2012), you were not eligible to make contributions, and until last year, if your modified adjusted gross income (MAGI) was over $100,000 (single or joint), you could not convert a traditional IRA to a Roth. Outside these contribution limits, most people save for retirement through their employers and most employers do not offer Roth options in their plans. The reason behind this is because Roth accounts are not that well understood and people have been educated to believe that saving on taxes today is the best possible course of action.

TAX-ADVANTAGED MONEY: LIFE INSURANCE

As previously mentioned, the single greatest tax asset that has come from Congress outside of life insurance is the Roth account. Life insurance is the little-known or little-discussed tax asset that holds some of the greatest value in your financial history both during life and upon death. It is by far the best tax-advantaged device available. We traditionally view life insurance as a way to protect our loved ones from financial ruin upon our demise and it should be noted that everyone who cares about someone should have life insurance. Purchasing a life insurance policy ensures that our loved ones will receive income from the life insurance company to help them pay our final expenses and carry on their lives without us comfortably when we die. The best part of the life insurance windfall is the fact that nobody will have to pay tax on the money received. This is the single greatest tax-advantaged device available, but it has one downside, we do not get to use it. Only our heirs will.

The little known and discussed part of life insurance is the cash value build-up within whole life and universal life (permanent) policies. Life insurance is not typically seen as an investment vehicle for building wealth and retirement planning, although we should discuss briefly why this thought process should be re-evaluated. Permanent life insurance is generally misconceived as something that is very expensive for a wealth accumulation vehicle because there are mortality charges (fees for the death benefit) that detract from the available returns. Furthermore, those returns do not yield as much as the stock market over the long run. This is why many times you will hear the phrase "buy term and invest the rest," where "term" refers to term insurance.

Let us take a second to review two terms just used in regard to life insurance: term and permanent. Term insurance is an idea with which most people are familiar. You purchase a certain death benefit that will go to your heirs upon death and this policy will be in effect for a certain number of years, typically 10 to 20 years. The 10 to 20 years is the term of the policy and once you have reached that end you no longer have insurance unless you purchase another policy.

Permanent insurance on the other hand has no term involved. It is permanent as long as the premiums continue to be paid. Permanent insurance generally initially has higher premiums than term insurance for the same amount of death benefit coverage and it is this difference that is referred to when people say "invest the rest."

Simply speaking there are significant differences between these two policies that are not often considered when providing a comparative analysis of the numbers. One item that gets lost in the fray when comparing term and permanent insurance is that term usually expires before death. In fact, insurance studies show less than one percent of all term policies pay out death benefit claims. The issue arises when the term expires and the desire to have more insurance is still present.

A term policy with the same benefit will be much more expensive than the original policy and, many times, life events occur, such as cancer or heart conditions, which makes it impossible to acquire another policy and leaves your loved ones unprotected and tax-advantaged legacy planning out of the equation.

Another aspect and probably the most important piece in consideration of the future of taxation is the fact that permanent insurance has a cash accumulation value. Two aspects stand out with the cash accumulation value. First, as the cash accumulation value increases the death benefit will also increase whereas term insurance remains level. Second, this cash accumulation offers value to you during your lifetime rather than to your heirs upon death. The cash accumulation value can be used for tax-advantaged income during your lifetime through policy loans. Most importantly, this tax-advantaged income is available during retirement for distribution planning, all while offering the same typical financial protection to your heirs.

TAX-DEFERRED MONEY

Tax-deferred money is the type of money with which most of people are familiar, but we also briefly reviewed the idea above. Tax-deferred money is typically our traditional IRA, employer sponsored retirement plan or a non-qualified annuity. Essentially, you put money into an investment vehicle that will accumulate in value over time and you do not pay taxes on the earnings that grow these accounts until you distribute them. Once the money is distributed, taxes must be paid. However, the same negative consequences exist with regard to additional taxation and expense in other areas as previously discussed. The cash accumulation value can be used for tax-advantaged income.

TAXABLE MONEY

Taxable money is everything else and is taxable today, later or whenever it is received. These four types of money come down to two distinct classifications: taxable and tax-free. The greatest difference when comparing taxable and tax-advantaged income is a function of how much money we keep after tax. For help in determining what the differences should be, excluding outside factors such as Social Security taxation and AMT, a tax equivalent yield should be used.

TAX-ADVANTAGED IN THE REAL WORLD

To put the tax equivalent yield into perspective, let us look at an example: Bob and Mary are currently retired, living on Social Security and interest from investments and falling within the 25 percent tax bracket. They have a substantial portion of their investments in municipal bonds yielding 6 percent, which is quite comforting in today's market. The tax equivalent yield they would need to earn from a taxable investment would be 8 percent, a 2 percent gap that seems almost impossible given current market volatility. However, something that has never been put into perspective is that the interest from their municipal bonds is subject to taxation on their Social Security benefits (at 21.25 percent). With this, the yield on their municipal bonds would be 4.725 percent, and the taxable equivalent yield falls to 6.3 percent, leaving a gap of only 1.575 percent.

In the end, most people spend their lives accumulating wealth through the best, if not the only vehicle they know, a tax-deferred account. This account is most likely a 401(k) or 403(b) plan offered through our employer and may be supplemented with an IRA that was established at one point or another. As the years go by, people blindly throw money into these accounts in an effort to save for a retirement that we someday hope to reach.

The truth is, most people have an age selected for when they would like to retire, but spend their lives wondering if they will ever be able to actually quit working. To answer this question, you must understand how much money you will have available to contribute toward your needs. *In other words, you need to know what your after-tax income will be during this period.*

All else being equal, it would not matter if you put your money into a taxable, tax-deferred or tax-advantaged account as long as income tax rates never change and outside factors are never an event. The net amount you receive in the end will be the same. Unfortunately, this will never be the case. We already know that taxes will increase in the future, meaning we will likely see higher taxes in retirement than during our peak earning years.

Regardless, saving for retirement in any form is a good thing as it appears from all practical perspectives that future government benefits will be cut and taxes will increase. You have the ability to plan today for efficient tax diversification and maximization of our after-tax dollars during your distribution years.

13

BEYOND A BALANCE: YOUR LEGACY

If you're like most people, planning your estate isn't on the top of your list of things to do. Planning your income needs for retirement, managing your assets and just living your life without worrying about how your estate will be handled when you are gone make legacy planning less than attractive for a Saturday afternoon task. The fact of the matter, however, is that if you don't plan your legacy, someone else will. That someone else is usually a combination of the IRS and other government entities: lawyers, executors, courts, and accountants. Who do you think has the best interests of your beneficiaries in mind?

Today, there is more consideration given to planning a legacy than just maximizing your estate. When most people think about an estate, it may seem like something only the very wealthy have: a stately manor or an enormous business. But a legacy is something else entirely. A legacy is more than the sum total of the financial assets you have accumulated. It is the lasting impression you make on those you leave behind. The dollar and cents are just a small part of a legacy.

A legacy encompasses the stories that others tell about you, shared experiences and values. An estate may pay for college tuition, but a legacy may inform your grandchildren about the importance of higher education and self-reliance.

A legacy may also contain family heirlooms or items of emotional significance. It may be a piece of art your great-grandmother painted, family photos, or a childhood keepsake.

When you go about planning your legacy, certainly explore strategies that can maximize the financial benefit to the ones you care about. But also take the time to ensure that you have organized the whole of your legacy, and let that be a part of the last gift you leave.

Many people avoid planning their legacy until they feel they must.

Something may change in your life, like the birth of a grandchild, the diagnosis of a serious health problem, or the death of a close friend or loved one. Waiting for tragedy to strike in order to get your affairs in order is not the best course of action. The emotional stress of that kind of situation can make it hard to make patient, thoughtful decisions. Taking the time to create a premeditated and thoughtful legacy plan will assure that your assets will be transferred where and when you want them when the time comes.

THE BENEFITS OF PLANNING YOUR LEGACY

The distribution of your assets, whether in the form of property, stocks, Individual Retirement Accounts, 401(k)s, TSPs or liquid assets, can be a complicated undertaking if you haven't left clear instructions about how you want them handled. Not having a plan will cost more money and take more time, leaving your loved ones to wait (sometimes for years) and receive less of your legacy than if you had a clear plan.

Planning your legacy will help your assets be transferred with little delay and little confusion. Instead of leaving decisions about how to distribute your estate to your family, attorneys or financial professionals, preserve your legacy and your wishes by drafting a clear plan at an early age.

And while you know all that, it can still be hard to sit down and do it. It reminds you that life is short, and the relatively complicated nature of sorting through your assets can feel like a daunting task. But one thing is for sure: *it is impossible for your assets to be transferred or distributed the way you want at the end of your life if you don't have a plan.*

Ask yourself:

- Are the beneficiary designations on my assets up to date?
- Have my primary and contingent beneficiaries been clearly designated?
- Does my plan allow for restriction of a beneficiary?
- Does my legacy plan address minor children that I want to provide with income?
- Does my legacy plan allow for multi-generational payout?

Answers to these questions are critical if you want the final say in how your assets are distributed. In order to achieve your legacy goals, you need a plan.

MAKING A PLAN

Eventually, when your income need is filled and you have sufficient standby money to meet your need for emergencies, travel or other extra expenses you are planning for, whatever isn't used during your lifetime becomes your financial legacy. The money that you do not use during your lifetime will either go to loved ones, unloved ones, charity, or the IRS. The questions is, who would you rather disinherit?

By having a legacy plan that clearly outlines your assets, your beneficiaries and your distribution goals, you can make sure that your money and property is ending up in the hands of the people you determine beforehand. Is it really that big of a deal? It absolutely is. Think about it. Without a clear plan, it is impossible for anyone to know if your beneficiary designations are current and reflect your wishes because you haven't clearly expressed who your beneficiaries are. You may have an idea of who you want your assets to go to, but without a plan, it is anyone's guess. It is also impossible to know if the titling of your assets is accurate unless you have gone through and determined whose name is on the titles. More importantly, *if you have not clearly and effectively communicated your desires regarding the planned distribution of your legacy, you and your family may end up losing a large part of it.*

As you can see, managing a legacy is more complicated than having an attorney read your will, divide your estate and write checks to your heirs. The additional issue of taxes, Family Maximum Benefit calculations and a host of other decisions rear their heads. Educating yourself about the best options for positioning your legacy assets is a challenging undertaking. Working with a financial professional who is versed in determining the most efficient and effective ways of preserving and distributing your legacy can save you time, money and strife.

So, how do you begin?

Making a Legacy Plan Starts with a Simple List. The first, and one of the largest, steps to setting up an estate plan with a financial professional that reflects your desires is creating a detailed inventory of your assets and debts (if you have any). You need to know what assets you have, who the beneficiaries are, how much they are worth and how they are titled. You can start by identifying and listing your assets. This is a good starting point for working with a financial professional who can then help you determine the detailed information about your assets that will dictate how they are distributed upon your death.

If you are particularly concerned about leaving your kids and grandkids a lifetime of income with minimal taxes, you will want to discuss a Stretch IRA option with your financial professional.

STRETCH IRAS: GETTING THE MOST OUT OF YOUR MONEY

In 1986, the U.S. Congress passed a law that allows for multi-generational distributions of IRA assets. This type of distribution is called a Stretch IRA because it stretches the distribution of the account out over a longer period of time to several beneficiaries. It also allows the account to continue accumulating value throughout your relatives' lifetimes. You can use a Stretch IRA as an income tool that distributes throughout your lifetime, your children's lifetimes and your grandchildren's lifetimes.

Stretch IRAs are an attractive option for those more concerned with creating income for their loved ones than leaving them with a lump sum that may be subject to a high tax rate. With traditional IRA distributions, non-spousal beneficiaries must generally take distributions from their inherited IRAs, whether transferred or not, within five years after the death of the IRA owner. An exception to this rule applies if the beneficiary elects to take distributions over his or her lifetime, which is referred to as stretching the IRA.

Let's begin by looking at the potential of stretching an IRA across multiple generations.

» *In this scenario, Mr. Cleaver has an IRA with a current balance of $350,000. If we assume a five percent annual rate of return, and a 28 percent tax rate, the Stretch IRA turned a $502,625 legacy into more than $1.5 million. Doubling the value of the IRA also provided Mr. Cleaver, his wife, two children and three grandchildren with income. Not choosing the stretch option would have cost nearly $800,000 and had impacts on six of Mr. Cleaver's loved ones.*

Unfortunately, many things may also play a role in failing to stretch IRA distributions. It can be tempting for a beneficiary to take a lump sum of money despite the tax consequences. Fortunately, if you want to solidify your plan for distribution, there are options that will allow you to open up an IRA and incorporate "spendthrift" clauses for your beneficiaries. This will ensure your legacy is stretched appropriately and to your specifications. Only certain insurance companies allow this option, and you will not find this benefit with any brokerage accounts. You need to work with a financial professional who has the appropriate relationship with an insurance company that provides this option.

14

HOW TO CREATE A LEGACY

David organized his assets long ago. He started planning his retirement early and made investment decisions that would meet his needs. With a combination of IRA to Roth IRA conversions, a series of income annuities and a well-planned money management strategy overseen by his financial professional, he easily filled his income gap and was able to focus on ways to accumulate his wealth throughout his retirement. He reorganized his Know So and Hope So Money as he got older. When David retired, he had an income plan created that allowed him to maximize his Social Security benefit. He even had enough to accumulate wealth during his retirement. At this point, David turned his attention to planning his legacy. He wanted to know how he could maximize the amount of his legacy he will pass on to his heirs.

David met with an attorney to draw up a will, but he quickly learned that while having a will was a good plan, it wasn't the most efficient way to distribute his legacy. In fact, relying solely on a will created several issues.

The two main problems that arose for David were *Probate* and *Unintentional Disinheritance*:

Problem #1: Probate

Probate. Just speaking the word out loud can cause shivers to run down your spine. Probate's ugly reputation is well deserved. It can be a costly, time consuming process that diminishes your estate and can delay the distribution of your estate to your loved ones. Nasty stuff, by any measure. Unless you have made a clear legacy plan and discussed options for avoiding probate, it is highly likely that you have many assets that might pass through probate needlessly. ***If your will and beneficiary designations aren't correctly structured, some of these assets will go through the probate process, which can turn dollars into cents.***

If you have a will, probate is usually just a formality. There is little risk that your will won't be executed per your instructions. The problem arises when the costs and lengthy timeline that probate creates come into play. Probate proceedings are notoriously expensive, lengthy and ponderous. A typical probate process identifies all of your assets and debts, pays any taxes and fees that you owe (including estate tax), pays court fees, and distributes your property and assets to your heirs. This process usually takes at least a year, and can take even longer before your heirs actually receive anything that you have left for them. For this reason, and because of the sometimes exorbitant fees that may be charged by lawyers and accountants during the process, probate has earned a nasty reputation.

Probate can also be a painstakingly public process. Because the probate process happens in court, the assets you own that go through a probate procedure become part of the public record.

While this may not seem like a big deal to some, other people don't want that kind of intimate information available to the public.

Additionally, if your estate is entirely distributed via your will, the money that your family may need to cover the costs of your medical bills, funeral expenses and estate taxes will be tied up in probate, which can last up to a year or more. While immediate family members may have the option of requesting immediate cash from your assets during probate to cover immediate health care expenses, taxes, and fees, that process comes with its own set of complications. Choosing alternative methods for distributing your legacy can make life easier for your loved ones and can help them claim more of your estate in a more timely fashion than traditional methods.

A simpler and less tedious approach is to avoid probate altogether by structuring your estate to be distributed outside of the probate process. Two common ways of doing this are by structuring your assets inside a life insurance plan, and by using individual retirement planning tools like IRAs that give you the option of designating a beneficiary upon your death.

Problem #2: Unintentionally Disinheriting Your Family

You would never want to unintentionally disinherit a loved one or loved ones because of confusion surrounding your legacy plan. Unfortunately, it happens. Why? This terrible situation is typically caused by a simple lack of understanding. In particular, mistakes regarding legacy distribution occur with regards to those whom people care for the most: their grandchildren.

One of the most important ways to plan for the inheritance of your grandchildren is by properly structuring the distribution of your legacy. Specifically, you need to know if your legacy is going to be distributed *per stirpes* or *per capita*.

Per Stirpes. *Per stirpes* is a legal term in Latin that means "by the branch." Your estate will be distributed *per stirpes* if you designate each branch of your family to receive an equal share of your estate. In the event that your children predecease you, their share will be distributed evenly between their children — your grandchildren.

Per Capita. *Per capita* distribution is different in that you may designate different amounts of your estate to be distributed to members of the same generation.

Per stirpes distribution of assets will follow the family tree down the line as the predecessor beneficiaries pass away. On the other hand, per capita distribution of assets ends on the branch of the family tree with the death of a designated beneficiary. For example, when your child passes away, in a per capita distribution, your grandchildren would not receive distributions from the assets that you designated to your child.

What the terms mean is not nearly as important as what they do, however. The reality is that improperly titled assets could accidentally leave your grandchildren disinherited upon the death of their parents. It's easy to check, and it's even easier to fix.

A simple way to remember the difference between the two types of distribution goes something like this: *"**Stirpes are forever and Capita is capped.**"*

Another way to avoid complicated legacy distribution problems, and the probate process, is by leveraging a life insurance plan.

LIFE INSURANCE: AN IMPORTANT LEGACY TOOL

One of the most powerful legacy tools you can leverage is a good life insurance policy. Life insurance is a highly efficient legacy tool because it creates money when it is needed or desired the most. Over the years, life insurance has become less expensive, while it offers more features, and it provides longer guarantees.

There are many unique benefits of life insurance that can help your beneficiaries get the most out of your legacy. Some of them include:

- Providing beneficiaries with a tax-free, liquid asset.
- Covering the costs associated with your death.
- Providing income for your dependents.
- Offering an investment opportunity for your beneficiaries.
- Covering expenses such as tuition or mortgage down payments for your children or grandchildren.

> **Very few people want life insurance, but nearly everyone wants what it does.**

Life insurance is specifically, and uniquely, capable of creating money when it is needed most. When a loved one passes, no amount of money can remove the pain of loss. And certainly, money doesn't solve the challenges that might arise with losing someone important.

It has been said that when you have money, you have options. When you don't have money, your options are severely limited. You might imagine a life insurance policy can give your family and loved ones options that would otherwise be impossible.

» *Ben spent the last 20 years building a small business. In so many ways, it is a family business. Each of his three children, Maddie, Ruby and Edward, worked in the shop part-time during high school. But after all three attended college, only Maddie returned to join her father, and eventually will run the business full-time when Ben retires.*

Ben is able to retire comfortably on Social Security and on-going income from the shop, but the business is nearly his entire financial legacy. It is his wish that Maddie own the business outright, but he also wants to leave an equal legacy to each of his three children.

There is no simple way to divide the business into thirds and still leave the business intact for Maddie.

Ben ends up buying a life insurance policy to make up the difference. Ruby and Edward will receive their share of an inheritance in cash from the life insurance policy and Maddie will be able to inherit the business intact.

Ben is able to accomplish his goals, treat all three children equitably and leave Maddie the business she helped to build.

If you have a life insurance policy but you haven't looked at it in a while, you may not know how it operates, how much it is worth and how it will be distributed to your beneficiaries. You may also need to update your beneficiaries on your policy. In short, without a comprehensive review of your policy, you don't really know where the money will go or to whom it will go.

If you don't have a life insurance policy but are looking for options to maintain and grow your legacy, speaking with a professional can show you the benefits of life insurance. Many people don't consider buying a life insurance policy until some event in their life triggers it, like the loss of a loved one, an accident or a health condition.

BENEFITS OF LIFE INSURANCE

Life insurance is a useful and secure tool for contingency planning, ensuring that your dependents receive the assets that you want them to have, and for meeting the financial goals you have set for the future. While it bears the name "Life Insurance," it is, in reality, a diverse financial tool that can meet many needs. The main function of a life insurance policy is to provide financial assets for your survivors. Life insurance is particularly efficient at achieving this goal because it provides a tax-advantaged lump sum of money in the form of a death benefit to your beneficiary or beneficiaries. That financial asset can be used in a number of ways. It can be structured as an investment to provide income for your spouse or children, it can pay down debts, and it can be used to cover estate taxes and other costs associated with death.

Tax liabilities on the estate you leave behind are inevitable. Capital property, for instance, is taxed at its fair market value at the time of your death, unless that property is transferred to your spouse. If the property has appreciated during the time you owned it, taxation on capital gains will occur. Registered Retirement Savings Plans (RRSPs) and other similarly structured assets are also included as taxable income unless transferred to a beneficiary as well. Those are just a few examples of how an estate can become subject to a heavy tax burden. The unique benefits of a life insurance policy provide ways to handle this tax burden, solving any liquidity problems that may arise if your family members want to hold onto an illiquid asset, such as a piece of property or an investment. Life insurance can provide a significant amount of money to a family member or other beneficiary, and that money is likely to remain exempt from taxation or seizure.

One of life insurance's most important benefits is that it is not considered part of the estate of the policy holder. The death benefit that is paid by the insurance company goes exclusively to the beneficiaries listed on the policy. This shields the proceeds of the policy from fees and costs that can reduce an estate, including probate proceedings, attorneys' fees and claims made by creditors. The distribution of your life insurance policy is also unaffected by delays of the estate's distribution, like probate. Your beneficiaries will get the proceeds of the policy in a timely fashion, regardless of how long it takes for the rest of your estate to be settled.

Investing a portion of your assets in a life insurance policy can also protect that portion of your estate from creditors. If you owe money to someone or some entity at the time of your death, a creditor is not able to claim any money from a life insurance policy or an annuity, for that matter. As an exception to this rule, if you had already used the life insurance policy as collateral against a loan. If a large portion of the money you want to dedicate to your legacy is sitting in a savings account, investment or other liquid form, creditors may be able to receive their claim on it before your beneficiaries get anything - that is, if there's anything left. A life insurance policy protects your assets from creditors and ensures that your beneficiaries get the money that you intend them to have.

HOW MUCH LIFE INSURANCE DO YOU NEED?

Determining the type of policy and the amount right for you depends on an analysis of your needs. A financial professional can help you complete a needs analysis that will highlight the amount of insurance that you require to meet your goals. This type of personalized review will allow you to determine ways to continue providing income for your spouse or any dependents you may have. A financial professional can also help you calculate the amount of income that your policy should replace to meet the needs of your beneficiaries and the duration of the distribution of that income.

You may also want to use your life insurance policy to meet any expenses associated with your death. These can include funeral costs, fees from probate and legal proceedings, and taxes. You may also want to dedicate a portion of your policy proceeds to help fund tuition or other expenses for your children or grandchildren. You can buy a policy and hope it covers all of those costs, or you can work with a professional who can calculate exactly how much insurance you need and how to structure it to meet your goals. Which would you rather do?

AVOIDING POTENTIAL SNAGS

There are benefits to having life insurance supersede the direction given in a will or other estate plan, but there are also some potential snags that you should address to meet your wishes. For example, if your will instructs that your assets be divided equally between your two children but your life insurance beneficiary is listed as just one of the children, the assets in the life insurance policy will only be distributed to the child listed as the beneficiary. The beneficiary designation of your life insurance supersedes your will's instruction. This is important to understand when designating beneficiaries on a policy you purchase. Work with a professional to make sure that your beneficiaries are accurately listed on your assets, especially your life insurance policies.

USING LIFE INSURANCE TO BUILD YOUR LEGACY

A couple of years ago, a doctor, Jackson, attended one of our workshops. That day, he made an appointment for him and his wife, Renee, to meet us, and they came in the next week. That began a focused session of meetings, about 10 over a year, during which we helped Jackson and Renee shape their retirement and legacy dreams. One of those dreams was to leave an endowment for the university where Renee was a professor.

One option, we told them, is to simply write a check for whatever amount you want (and can afford) to contribute. But then we showed them an even better option: life insurance.

We wrote a life insurance policy in which the endowment owns the policy; Jackson and Renee pay a premium every year of $50,000 for ten years then it is paid in full. When the life insurance policy pays out, the endowment will be paid $2 million. They will end up giving much more to the university than they could have afforded out of pocket and the legacy of all of the work Renee has done at that institution will be safeguarded. What's more, we set up the policy *so that their premiums are tax deductible donations that save them about $15,000 each year.*

Jackson and Renee's policy was also a second to die policy, which means that the policy only pays out when the second one passes away. By having them both on the policy—Renee being in better health— they were able to get a higher value.

Depending on your goals, there are strategies you can use that could multiply how much you leave behind. Life insurance is one of the most surefire and efficient investment tools for building a substantial legacy that will meet your financial goals.

Here is a brief overview of how life insurance can boost your legacy:

- Life insurance provides an immediate increase in your legacy.
- It provides an income tax-advantaged death benefit for your beneficiaries.
- A good life insurance policy has the opportunity to accumulate value over time.
- It may have an option to include long-term care (LTC) or chronic illness benefits should you require them.

If your Green Money income needs for retirement are met and you have Yellow Money assets that will provide for your future expenses, you may have extra assets that you want to earmark as legacy funds. By electing to invest those assets into a life insurance policy, you can immediately increase the amount of your legacy. Remember, **life insurance allows you to transfer a tax-advantaged lump sum of money to your beneficiaries. It remains in your control during your lifetime, can provide for your long-term care needs and bypasses probate costs.** And make no mistake, taxes can have a huge impact on your legacy.

Not only that, income and assets from your legacy can have tax implications for your beneficiaries, as well.

Here's a brief overview of how taxes could affect your legacy and your beneficiaries:

- The higher your income, the higher the rate at which it is taxed.
- Withdrawals from qualified plans are taxed as income.
- What's more, when you leave a large qualified plan, it ends up being taxed at a high rate.
- If you left a $500,000 IRA to your child, they could end up owing as much as $140,000 in income taxes.
- However, if you could just withdraw $50,000 a year, the tax bill might only be $10,000 per year.

How could you use that annual amount to leave a larger legacy? Luckily, you can leverage a life insurance policy to avoid those tax penalties, preserving a larger amount of your legacy and freeing your beneficiaries from an added tax burden.

When Brenda turned 70 years old, she decided it was time to look into life insurance policy options. She still feels young, but she remembers that her mother died in early 70s, and she wants to plan ahead so she can pass on some of her legacy to her grandchildren just like her grandmother did for her.

Brenda doesn't really want to think about life insurance, but she does want the security, reliability and tax-advantaged distribution that it offers. She lives modestly, and her Social Security benefit meets most of her income needs. As the beneficiary of her late husband's Certificate of Deposit (CD), she has $100,000 in an account that she has never used and doesn't anticipate ever needing since her income needs were already met.

*After looking at several different investment options with a professional, Brenda decides that a Single Premium life insurance policy fits her needs best. She can buy the policy with a $100,000 one-time payment and she is guaranteed that it would provide more than the value of the contract to her beneficiaries. If she left the money in the CD, it would be subject to taxes. But for every dollar that she puts into the life insurance policy, her beneficiaries are guaranteed at least that dollar plus a death benefit, and all of it will be **tax-free!***

For $100,000, Brenda's particular policy offers a $170,000 death benefit distribution to her beneficiaries. By moving the $100,000 from a CD to a life insurance policy, Brenda increases her legacy by 70 percent. Not only that, she has also sheltered it from taxes, so her beneficiaries will be able to receive $1.70 for every $1.00 that she entered into the policy! While buying the policy doesn't allow her to use the money for herself, it does allow her family to benefit from her well-planned legacy.

MAKE YOUR WISHES KNOWN

Estate taxes used to be a much hotter topic in the mid-2000s when the estate tax limits and exclusions were much smaller and taxed at a higher rate than today. In 2008, estates valued at $2 million or more were taxed at 45 percent. Just two years later, the limit was raised to $5 million dollars taxed at 35 percent. The limit has continued to rise ever since. The limit applies to fewer people than before. Estate organization, however, is just as important as ever, and it affects everyone.

Ask yourself:

- Are your assets actually titled and held the way you think they are?
- Are your beneficiaries set up the way you think they should be?

- Have there been changes to your family or those you desire as beneficiaries?

There is more to your legacy beyond your property, money, investments and other assets that you leave to family members, loved ones and charities. Everyone has a legacy beyond money. You also leave behind personal items of importance, your values and beliefs, your personal and family history, and your wishes. Beyond a will and a plan for your assets, it is important that you make your wishes known to someone for the rest of your personal legacy. When it comes time for your family and loved ones to make decisions after you are gone, knowing your wishes can help them make decisions that honor you and your legacy, and give meaning to what you leave behind. Your professional can help you organize.

Think about your:

- Personal stories/recollections
- Values
- Personal items of emotional significance
- Financial assets

Do you want to make a plan to pass these things on to your family?

WORKING WITH A PROFESSIONAL

Part of using life insurance to your greatest advantage is selecting the policy and provider that can best meet your goals. Venturing into the jungle of policies, brokers and salespeople can be overwhelming, and can leave you wondering if you've made the best decision. Working with a trusted financial professional can help you cut through the red tape, the "sales-speak" and confusion to find a policy that meets your goals and best serves your desires for your money. If you already have a policy, a financial professional can help you review it and become familiar with the policy's premium, the guarantees the policy affords, its performance, and its features and benefits. A financial professional can also help you make any necessary changes to the policy.

> » When Cheryl turned 88, her daughter finally convinced her to meet with a financial professional to help her organize her assets and get her legacy in order. Although Cheryl is reluctant to let a stranger in on her personal finances, she ends up very glad that she did.
>
> In the process of listing Cheryl's assets and her beneficiaries, her professional finds a man's name listed as the beneficiary of an old annuity that she owns. It turns out, the man is Cheryl's ex-husband who is still alive. Had Cheryl passed away before her ex-husband, the annuities and any death benefits that came with them, would have been passed on to her ex-husband. This does not reflect her latest wishes.

Things change, relationships evolve and the way you would like your legacy organized needs to adapt to the changes that happen throughout your life. There may be a new child or grandchild in your family, or you may have been divorced or remarried. A professional will regularly review your legacy assets and ask you questions to make sure that everything is up to date and that the current organization reflects your current wishes.

CHAPTER 14 RECAP //

- You can structure your assets in ways that maximize distributions to your beneficiaries.
- Working with a financial professional can help ensure that many of your assets avoid the ponderous and expensive probate process.
- A financial professional can help review the details of the assets you have designated to be a part of your legacy and make sure that you aren't unintentionally disinheriting your heirs.
- Life insurance provides the distribution of tax-free, liquid assets to your beneficiaries.
- Investing in a life insurance policy can significantly build your legacy.
- Organizing your estate will allow you to make sure your wishes are properly carried through.
- You can take advantage of a "Stretch IRA" to provide income for you, your spouse and your beneficiaries throughout their lifetimes.
- Understand if your assets will be distributed *per stirpes* or *per capita*.
- Working with a financial professional can help you select the policy that best meets your needs, or can help you fine tune your existing policy to better reflect your desires and intentions.

15

A LIVING TRUST, A LASTING LEGACY

LIVING TRUST

What is it?

A living trust (also known as a revocable living trust or inter vivos trust) is a separate legal entity that you create to own property, such as your home, boat, or investments. You transfer some or all of your property to the trust as soon as it is created. During your lifetime, you control the trust; you can change the trust terms, or terminate the trust and take the property back. At your death, the trust becomes irrevocable and may continue to exist for many years. The trustee administers and distributes the trust property according to the terms of the trust.

People create living trusts because they're able to retain control over their assets while achieving other important goals, such as:

- Controlling the manner and timing of asset distributions to heirs
- Efficiently transferring assets to heirs
- Enabling someone else to manage property
- Protecting property in case of incapacity
- Avoiding probate

Tip: Though a living trust is a separate legal entity, it is not a separate taxpayer during your lifetime. You are considered the owner of the trust assets for income tax purposes; all income, deductions, credits, and losses flow through to you. Upon your death, the trust becomes a separate taxpayer and different tax rules will apply (see Tax Considerations below).

Caution: A living trust does not avoid estate taxes and does not protect assets from potential future creditors. To attain these objectives, the trust must be irrevocable. For more information, see Tradeoffs below.

FUNDING THE TRUST

To ensure that the trust fulfills its objectives, the trust must be funded after it is created. Funding the trust means transferring legal title from the grantor into the name of the trust. This may entail recording a new deed for real estate; re-titling cars and trucks; renaming checking, savings, and investment portfolio accounts; transferring life insurance policies, stocks, and bonds; executing new beneficiary designation forms; or executing assignment.

Although a revocable living trust can be funded with virtually any kind of property, including personal property, special consideration should be made before transferring certain types of property, including:

- Incentive stock options
- Section 1244 (restricted) stock
- Professional corporations

Tip: Transfers to the trust are not considered gifts, so the grantor doesn't need to file a gift tax return.

Caution: Some states will reassess the value of a home for property tax purposes when it is transferred to a trust. Some states will disallow income tax deductions related to the home if it is owned by a trust.

Caution: Some banks may impose a penalty when certificates of deposits (CDs) are transferred to a trust because they consider such transfers to be early withdrawals.

WHEN CAN A LIVING TRUST BE USED?

Although a living trust can hold most types of property, it cannot hold:

- Qualified stock options or stock acquired under such a plan, at least until the holding period has passed
- An interest in a partnership, if prohibited by state law
- An interest in a cooperative or condominium, if prohibited by your contract with your co-owners
- An interest in a professional corporation (e.g., a law firm), because such an interest generally can only be owned by a professional (e.g., a lawyer)
- An IRA, although you can name your living trust as beneficiary of your IRA

SUITABLE LIVING TRUST CLIENTS

A revocable living trust can be appropriate for individuals:

- Owning real estate in more than one state (to avoid ancillary probate)
- With concerns about their health or future ability to manage their own financial affairs
- Who want to keep transfers at death private (to avoid family conflicts, for example)
- Who want someone else to manage and invest assets (e.g., persons with special needs, persons who often travel overseas)
- Who want someone with special knowledge or skill to manage and invest assets (e.g., persons who inherit or win large sums of money)
- Who are single or who care for themselves
- Who are unmarried domestic partners
- Who are elderly or ill
- Who are not concerned about transfer taxes

» *Joseph and Margaret just celebrated their golden wedding anniversary. They have a 49-year-old daughter, Kathleen, who is a professor at the community college, and a 47-year-old son, Daniel, who is an engineer. Joseph›s health is beginning to fail, and lately, he›s had a little trouble remembering things. Joseph has always taken care of the family finances, and he›s worried that Margaret might not be able to manage them on her own if something should happen to him. Joseph and Margaret own the following assets jointly:*
- *Home: $600,000*
- *Checking and savings accounts: $2,000*
- *Certificates of deposit (CDs): $20,000*
- *Bonds: $7,000*
- *Mutual funds: $5,500*
- *Life insurance: $1 million*
- *Total: $1,634,500*

Joseph and Margaret aren›t worried about federal transfer taxes because their estates ($817,250 each) will be sheltered by their exemptions ($5,340,000 per individual in 2014). So, Joseph and Margaret transfer all of the couple›s assets to a revocable living trust.

Joseph is named as trustee and his daughter, Kathleen, is named as successor trustee. The trust also names Daniel as successor trustee if Kathleen cannot serve for some reason. The sole beneficiaries of the trust during their lives will be Joseph and Margaret, and, upon the death of the last spouse to die, any assets remaining in the trust will pass to Kathleen and Daniel equally.

Now, Joseph can still manage the couple›s property himself, but knows that if he should become incapacitated or die before Margaret, Kathleen (and if not Kathleen, Daniel) will immediately take charge, paying the bills and providing Wilma with income until she dies. Joseph also knows that when Margaret dies, Kathleen and Daniel will receive their inheritances without the delay and costs of probate.

ADVANTAGES

Lets you control your property until your death
A living trust is revocable until your death. That means you can use or withdraw trust property, change the trust terms, add or remove beneficiaries, replace the trustee, or even revoke the trust entirely up until your death. This gives you flexibility to meet unknown future contingencies and still meet other goals.

Allows distribution of your property to be customized
A will generally transfers specific amounts or percentages of your property to your beneficiaries. By placing your property in a living trust, you can direct the trustee to distribute property only

in certain situations, for example "to pay tuition," or on certain occasions such as "on my son's 30th birthday," or at the trustee's discretion, perhaps "to my children, as necessary to fund their educational needs."

This may be beneficial if you're worried your heirs may be unable to manage outright gifts, or if you want to create "rewards" for certain behaviors.

> **Caution:** Although a trust transfers property like a will, you should still have a will as well because the trust will be unable to accomplish certain things that only a will can, such as naming an executor or a guardian for minor children.

Minimizes delays in the transfer of property

Probate takes time and your property generally won't be distributed until the process is completed. A small family allowance is sometimes paid, but it may be insufficient to provide for a family's ongoing needs. Transferring property through a living trust provides for a quicker, almost immediate transfer of property to those who need it.

Probate can also interfere with the management of property like a closely held business or stock portfolio. Although your executor is responsible for managing the property until probate is completed, he or she may not have the expertise or authority to make significant management decisions, and the property may lose value. Transferring the property with a living trust can result in a smoother transition in management.

Circumvents some limits on your power to transfer property

State law may limit your ability to leave property to charity. For example, some states invalidate any bequest to charity written within a month of your death. Other states won't let you leave more than a certain percentage of your property to charity. These laws often don't apply to living trusts.

State law may also force you to leave a certain percentage of your property to your spouse. In some states, these laws don't apply to living trusts.

Lets someone else manage your property for you

You may find that managing certain property is a burden, or that you do not possess the skills required to manage certain property competently. Or, you may be planning to be away from home for a period of time and unable to make financial decisions or transact certain business. Or, you may be entering public service and need to avoid the appearance of a conflict of interest. A living trust lets you name someone who can successfully handle your financial affairs for you in these situations.

Gives someone the power to manage your property if you become incapacitated

If incapacity strikes, your trustee (or a co-trustee if you are the trustee) can take immediate control of your property to use it for your care and support, or in whatever way you have directed by the terms of the trust. This may help avoid the potential need for guardianship.

Avoids probate

Because property in a living trust is not included in the probate estate, some people may use them to avoid probate. Depending on your situation and your state's laws, the probate process can be simple, easy, and inexpensive or it can be relatively complex, resulting in delay and expense. This may be the case, for instance, if you own property in more than one state or in a foreign country, or have heirs that live overseas.

Avoiding probate may also be desirable if you are concerned about privacy. Probated documents (e.g., will, inventory) become a matter of public record. Generally, a trust document does not.

On the other hand, the probate process can serve many important functions, such as protecting the interests of beneficiaries and resolving disputes.

Determining whether avoiding probate would be advantageous, then, depends on many factors.

> **Tip:** There are other ways to avoid the probate process other than using a living trust, such as titling property jointly.

TRADEOFFS

You may incur attorney's fees to create
A living trust is a sophisticated legal document that should be drafted by a competent attorney who understands your state's laws as well as your personal situation and objectives. An attorney will help you coordinate your trust with other estate planning and financial goals, and will advise you regarding how to effectively execute and fund this device.

> **Caution:** Though there are "do-it-yourself" living trust kits available, you take many risks if you use one of these "one-size-fits-all" forms. It may end up costing you more if the trust is the wrong form, a form that is not valid in your state, is not appropriately customized to your situation, is not properly executed, or is not properly funded.

Funding the trust can be burdensome and costly
In order to be effective, you must transfer title to property being transferred to the trust. This can be complicated and burdensome,

though your attorney will offer advice to help you. Transferring some types of property can be especially difficult and costly:

- **Real estate:** Some states assess a transfer tax or reassess property taxes whenever real property changes hands, even if it is only being transferred to a living trust. In other states, homeowner tax deductions are not available if the land is owned by a living trust.
- **Secured or insured property:** If property secures a loan, that loan may prohibit any transfer of the property, even to a living trust. Title or property insurance may also prohibit transfer of the property to the trust.

Should not be used to transfer some types of property

Although a living trust can hold most types of property, it is generally inappropriate for the following types of property:

- Stock acquired at less than market value under a restricted stock option or stock purchase plan, because income tax will be assessed on the gain
- Certificate of deposit, because of the penalty that will result if the bank considers the transfer an early withdrawal
- Real estate generating loss, since you probably cannot take losses on actively managed rental property owned by a living trust
- Personal property, such as furniture or clothing

Does not help achieve Medicaid eligibility

Assets in a revocable living trust are countable resources for the purposes of Medicaid eligibility. The assets are treated just as if you (the grantor) owned the them outright. Thus, your eligibility for Medicaid is reduced to reflect any gifts you make from your living trust during the preceding 60 months.

Caution: Questions regarding Medicaid eligibility are extremely complex. You should seek specific assistance with these issues.

Does not avoid estate taxes

Unlike an irrevocable trust, a living trust does not inherently reduce estate taxes. Because you retained control over the trust during your lifetime, property in the living trust at your death will be included in your gross estate for estate tax purposes, even though they won't be considered part of your estate for probate purposes.

Tip: Spouses can use a special living trust (i.e., a bypass or credit shelter trust) to help minimize estate taxes on their combined estates. With such a trust, both spouses can more fully utilize their applicable exclusion amounts. However, you do not need a living trust to accomplish this; you can create the bypass trust at your death by including a pourover provision in your will.

Does not protect property from creditors

The probate process requires that all claims against your estate be presented within months of your death, preventing delayed claims against your estate and beneficiaries. A creditor may be able to bring a claim against property that passed through your living trust for years after your death.

TAX CONSIDERATIONS

Income Tax

During your life

While you are living, the IRS will ignore the trust entity. All income, gains, losses, deductions, and credits flow through directly to you. Generally, you do not need to obtain a taxpayer identification number (TIN) for the trust, though you may choose to do so. You may furnish your own name and Social Security number to banks, brokers, and others paying income to the trust. You report all income on your own Form 1040 in the year it is earned, regardless of whether it was distributed to you. You do not need to file Form 1041. If you are not the trustee, however, the trustee must send you a statement with all pertinent information you will need to prepare your Form 1040.

You may choose to furnish banks, brokers, and others paying income to the trust with a TIN. In this case, the trustee must file Form 1099 and Form 1041. And, if you are not the trustee, the trustee must also send you a statement with all pertinent information you will need to prepare your Form 1040.

If you create a living trust jointly with your spouse, and you and your spouse file separate returns, you must use the second method described above.

After your death

If your living trust doesn't distribute all of the property it owns at your death, it becomes an irrevocable trust and is subject to income tax as a separate taxpayer. The tax rules become very complicated and are much less advantageous. Among other things, the trust:

- Cannot take a charitable deduction for income set aside for charity

- Must use a calendar tax year
- Cannot file a joint return with your surviving spouse in the year of your death
- Is allowed a smaller income tax exemption than for individuals
- Is subject to more compressed tax rates
- Cannot deduct losses on distributions of assets to beneficiaries
- Is assessed income tax on the gain if it takes ownership of stock acquired at less than market value under a restricted stock option or stock purchase plan
- Cannot take rental real estate losses
- May be unable to continue to hold S corporation stock after your death

A living trust can hold S corporation stock during your life without jeopardizing the corporation's S corporation status, as long as certain conditions are met. However, after you die, the trust is permitted to continue as a shareholder only for the two-year period beginning on the date of your death.

Caution: This is an extremely complex area. You should consult an experienced tax professional.

Gift and Estate Tax

- Must file gift tax returns when property is transferred to the trust
- Although transferring property to a living trust does not result in any gift tax liability (because transfers to a revocable trust are not "complete"), you are required to disclose the living trust on a gift tax return.
- Does not avoid estate taxes

- Because you retained control over the property during your lifetime, all property in your living trust at your death will be included in your estate for estate tax purposes, even though it is not included in your estate for probate purposes.

EPILOGUE:
LIVING YOUR
RETIREMENT DREAM

It's finally here! You've worked your last day. You've begun a whole new era in your life, one that's the result of years of planning. All of that planning, we hope, has resulted in a retirement that's comfortable, filled with all of the things you love and enjoy and allows to you to pass on whatever legacy you worked so hard to provide. But those things can only happen if you do this one last, crucial thing:

Stick to the plan.

As we discussed in the introduction, we help our clients structure their retirement around five key areas so that their personal finances will be insulated from the greater financial picture. One of those areas is the Uh-oh Fund, which allows for unanticipated costs, from needing a new transmission to deciding to take the grandkids on an Alaskan cruise.

> » *Bruce and Rhonda, two of our clients, had that Uh-oh Fund. And they used it. They really, really used it. First, they decided to buy an RV to travel to America's National Parks. Then they bought a new car. We support all of our clients travel dreams, and we know transportation is important. But what we DIDN'T know was that these purchases had taken place. By the time Bruce and Rhonda told us about these expenses, they had almost exhausted their Uh-oh Fund, which was structured to last the rest of their lives.*

There are two important lessons here. First, create a spending plan with your financial team, and stick to that plan. And second, if you have unexpected expenses or a life event— like marriage, new grandchildren, a major illness or other expense—let us know. Sometimes we will need to adjust how your finances are structured, and sometimes we won't. But the more we know, and the sooner we know, the more options we'll be able to offer you. And the more easily we can keep you kicked back, having fun and loving retirement.

When you choose to work with us, you take the first steps through the gateway that can help lead you to the retirement you deserve. Guided by your vision and our experience, we can help you design the plan that's right for you. To learn how you can begin living the retirement dream you've worked so hard for, visit our website at www.4lonestar.com.

ABOUT THE AUTHORS

MICHAEL JON BYERS, author, talk show host and financial planner

Michael Jon Byers is president and founder of Lonestar Registered Investment Advisors, PLLC and Texas Alliance Financial Services PLLC. Michael has a goal to help every client protect his or her personal financial life from a volatile market. It is Michael's mission to help educate and equip everyone to achieve the retirement of their dreams. As a well-known speaker, Michael is in high demand to teach financial literacy and employee benefits in the private sector as well as federal agencies. Michael has also spoken to many groups educating them on financial strategies and retirement planning.

Michael was an invited guest professor at Texas Tech University where he taught a class on macroeconomics. He has also been helping people avoid many of the pitfalls of planning a comfortable retirement for years. While speaking to thousands of people about planning their retirement, Michael has been able to expand his knowledge of the needs of the everyday investor. He is a familiar face on TV where he frequently contributes to news stories as a featured financial analyst. Michael's voice has been heard for over seven years as the host of a live, call-in radio show called "The Money Talk Show."

As an author, talk show host, and personal financial expert, Michael excels at helping making complex financial matters understandable for readers and audiences all over the country planning their retirement.

The proud son of an Army father, Michael grew up all over the world. In Korea, he attended a Korean preschool and spoke fluent Korean. While in Okinawa, Japan, he found his love of the beach and snorkeling with his Dad. Living in Germany for almost nine years, Michael enjoyed traveling most of Europe, and his love for travel has grown even more since then. In the United States, Michael has lived in the Maryland-Washington-DC area and currently lives in West Texas, one of the greatest places to raise a family. He stays busy growing his financial practice and raising four wonderful children, Kimberlee, Ethan, Caden and Seth. He enjoys the great outdoors and hunting with his kids. Michael also likes coaching or watching his children play the many sports they love.

MARK GROOM

Mark Groom graduated cum laude from Concordia College with dual majors in Business Administration and Spanish. Mark has a passion to help his clients prepare for retirement and offer solutions to help sustain their lifestyle throughout retirement. He has appeared on TV numerous times, offering analysis on various financial stories. For 7 years, he teamed up with Michael Byers on a live, call-in financial radio show called "The Money Talk Show."

For the past several years, Mark has taught various classes on budgeting and household money management at his local church. The main theme behind the classes is "Success is personal: financial planning doesn't just happen, it has to be intentional."

Mark grew up on a dairy farm in Minnesota where he learned the value of hard work. His father was a jet fighter pilot for 22 years while managing the dairy operation. That was hard work, but he is reaping the benefits today!

Being raised in a large family of five kids, Mark realized the value of working together, and appreciates and embraces the values and faith demonstrated to him by his parents.

PLANNING A SECURE RETIREMENT

Michael Jon Byers is available for speaking engagements and teaching how to start planning a secure retirement. If your group or federal agency would like to get more information about booking Michael Jon Byers as a keynote speaker at your next conference, training or meeting, please contact:

Maria Richburg
12402 Slide Road Suite 305
Lubbock Texas 79424

Email: Info@myalliancefinancial.com

Toll free: 1.866.785.5350

Or visit our websites:

www.4lonestar.com

www.planningasecureretirement.com

www.myalliancefinancial.com

GLOSSARY

ANNUAL RESET *(ANNUAL RATCHET, CLIQUET)* – Crediting methods measuring index movement over a one year period. Positive interest is calculated and credited at the end of each contract year and cannot be lost if the index subsequently declines. Say that the index increased from 100 to 110 in one year and the indexed annuity had an 80 percent participation rate. The insurance company would take the 10 percent gross index gain for the year (110-100/100), apply the participation rate (10 percent index gain x 80 percent rate) and credit 8 percent interest to the annuity. But, what if in the following year the index declined back to 100? The individual would keep the 8 percent interest earned and simply receive zero interest for the down year. An annual reset structure preserves credited gains and treats negative index periods as years with zero growth.

ANNUITANT – The person, usually the annuity owner, whose life expectancy is used to calculate the income payment amount on the annuity.

ANNUITY – An annuity is a contract issued by an insurance company that often serves as a type of savings plan used by individuals looking for long term growth and protection of assets that will likely be needed within retirement.

AVERAGING – Index values may either be measured from a start point to an end point (point-to-point) or values between the start point and end point may be averaged to determine an ending value. Index values may be averaged over the days, weeks, months or quarters of the period.

BENEFICIARY – A beneficiary is the person designated to receive payments due upon the death of the annuity owner or the annuitant themselves.

BONUS RATE – A bonus rate is the "extra" or "additional" interest paid during the first year (the initial guarantee period), typically used as an added incentive to get consumers to select their annuity policy over another.

CALL OPTION *(ALSO SEE PUT OPTION)* – Gives the holder the right to buy an underlying security or index at a specified price on or before a given date.

CAP – The maximum interest rate that will be credited to the annuity for the year or period. The cap usually refers to the maximum interest credited after applying the participation rate or yield spread. If the index methodology showed a 20 percent increase, the participation rate was 60 percent and the maximum interest cap was 10 percent, the contract would credit 10 percent interest. A few annuities use a maximum gain cap instead of a maximum interest cap with the participation rate or yield spread applied to the lesser of the gain or the cap. If the index methodology showed a 20 percent increase, the participation rate was 60 percent and the maximum gain cap was 10 percent, the contract would credit 6 percent interest.

COMPOUND INTEREST – Interest is earned on both the original principal and on previously earned interest. It is more favorable than simple interest. Suppose that your original principal was $1 and your interest rate was 10 percent for five years. With simple interest, your value is ($1 + $0.10 interest each year) = $1.50. With compound interest, your value is ($1 x 1.10 x 1.10 x 1.10

x 1.10 x 1.10) = $1.61. The advantage of compound interest over simple interest becomes greater as each subsequent period passes.

CREDITING METHOD *(ALSO SEE METHODOLOGY)* – The formula(s) used to determine the excess interest that is credited above the minimum interest guarantee.

DEATH BENEFITS – The payment the annuity owner's estate or beneficiaries will receive if he or she dies before the annuity matures. On most annuities, this is equal to the current account value. Some annuities offer an enhanced value at death via an optional rider that has a monthly or annual fee associated with it.

EXCESS INTEREST – Interest credited to the annuity contract above the minimum guaranteed interest rate. In an indexed annuity the excess interest is determined by applying a stated crediting method to a specific index or indices.

FIXED ANNUITY – A contract issued by an insurance company guaranteeing a minimum interest rate with the crediting of excess interest determined by the performance of the insurer's general account. Index annuities are fixed annuities.

FIXED DEFERRED ANNUITY – With fixed annuities, an insurance company offers a guaranteed interest rate plus safety of your principal and earnings ((subject to the claims-paying ability of the insurance company). Your interest rate will be reset periodically, based on economic and other factors, but is guaranteed to never fall below a certain rate.

FREE WITHDRAWALS – Withdrawals that are free of surrender charges.

INDEX – The underlying external benchmark upon which the crediting of excess interest is based, also a measure of the prices of a group of securities.

IRA *(INDIVIDUAL RETIREMENT ACCOUNT)* – An IRA is a tax-advantaged personal savings plan that lets an individual set aside money for retirement. All or part of the participant's contributions may be tax deductible, depending on the type of IRA chosen and the participant's personal financial circumstances. Distributions from many employer-sponsored retirement plans may be eligible to be rolled into an IRA to continue tax-deferred growth until the funds are needed. An annuity can be used as an IRA; that is, IRA funds can be used to purchase an annuity.

IRA ROLLOVER – IRA rollover is the phrase used when an individual who has a balance in an employer-sponsored retirement plan transfers that balance into an IRA. Such an exchange, when properly handled, is a tax-advantaged transaction.

LIQUIDITY – The ease with which an asset is convertible to cash. An asset with high liquidity provides flexibility, in that the owner can easily convert it to cash at any time, but it also tends to decrease profitability.

MARKET RISK – The risk of the market value of an asset fluctuating up or down over time. In a fixed or fixed indexed annuity, the original principal and credited interest are not subject to market risk. Even if the index declines, the annuity owner would receive no less than their original principal back if they decided to cash in the policy at the end of the surrender period. Unlike a security, indexed annuities guarantee the original premium and the premium is backed by, and is as safe as, the insurance company that issued it (subject to the claims-paying ability of the insurance company).

METHODOLOGY *(ALSO SEE CREDITING METHOD)* – The way that interest crediting is calculated. On fixed indexed annuities, there are a variety of different methods used to determine how index movement becomes interest credited.

MINIMUM GUARANTEED RETURN *(MINIMUM INTEREST RATE)* – Fixed indexed annuities typically provide a minimum guaranteed return over the life of the contract. At the time that the owner chooses to terminate the contract, the cash surrender value is compared to a second value calculated using the minimum guaranteed return and the higher of the two values is paid to the annuity owner.

OPTION – A contract which conveys to its holder the right, but not the obligation, to buy or sell something at a specified price on or before a given date. After this given date the option ceases to exist. Insurers typically buy options to provide for the excess interest potential. Options may be American style whereby they may be exercised at any time prior to the given date, or they may have to be exercised only during a specified window. Options that may only be exercised during a specified period are European-style options.

OPTION RISK – Most insurers create the potential for excess interest in an indexed annuity by buying options. Say that you could buy a share of stock for $50. If you bought the stock and it rose to $60 you could sell it and net a $10 profit. But, if the stock price fell to $40 you'd have a $10 loss. Instead of buying the actual stock, we could buy an option that gave us the right to buy the stock for $50 at any time over the next year. The cost of the option is $2. If the stock price rose to $60 we would exercise our option, buy the stock at $50 and make $10 (less the $2 cost of the option). If the price of the stock fell to $40, $30 or $10, we wouldn't use the option and it would expire. The loss is limited to $2 – the cost of the option.

PARTICIPATION RATE – The percentage of positive index movement credited to the annuity. If the index methodology determined that the index increased 10 percent and the indexed annuity participated in 60 percent of the increase, it would be said that the contract has a 60 percent participation rate. Participation rates may also be expressed as asset fees or yield spreads.

POINT-TO-POINT – A crediting method measuring index movement from an absolute initial point to the absolute end point for a period. An index had a period starting value of 100 and a period ending value of 120. A point-to-point method would record a positive index movement of 20 [120-100] or a 20 percent positive movement [(120-100)/100]. Point-to-point usually refers to annual periods; however the phrase is also used instead of term end point to refer to multiple year periods.

PREMIUM BONUS – A premium bonus is additional money that is credited to the accumulation account of an annuity policy under certain conditions.

PUT OPTION *(ALSO SEE CALL OPTION)* – Gives the holder the right to sell an underlying security or index at a specified price on or before a given date.

QUALIFIED ANNUITIES *(QUALIFIED MONEY)* – Qualified annuities are annuities purchased for funding an IRA, 403(b) tax-deferred annuity or other type of retirement arrangements. An IRA or qualified retirement plan provides the tax deferral. An annuity contract should be used to fund an IRA or qualified retirement plan to benefit from an annuity's features other than tax deferral, including the safety features, lifetime income payout option and death benefit protection.

REQUIRED MINIMUM DISTRIBUTION *(RMD)* – The amount of money that Traditional, SEP and SIMPLE IRA owners and qualified plan participants must begin distributing from their retirement accounts by April 1 following the year they reach age 70.5. RMD amounts must then be distributed each subsequent year.

RETURN FLOOR – Another way of saying minimum guaranteed return.

ROTH IRA – Like other IRA accounts, the Roth IRA is simply a holding account that manages your stocks, bonds, annuities, mutual funds and CD's. However, future withdrawals (including earnings and interest) are typically tax-advantaged once the account has been open for five years and the account holder is age 59.5.

RULE OF 72 – Tells you approximately how many years it takes a sum to double at a given rate. It's handy to be able to figure out, without using a calculator, that when you're earning a 6 percent return, for example, by dividing 6 percent into 72, you'll find that it takes 12 years for money to double. Conversely, if you know it took a sum twelve years to double you could divide 12 into 72 to determine the annual return (6 percent).

SIMPLE INTEREST *(ALSO SEE COMPOUND INTEREST)* – Interest is only earned on the principal balance.

SPLIT ANNUITY – A split annuity is the term given to an effective strategy that utilizes two or more different annuity products – one designed to generate monthly income and the other to restore the original starting principal over a set period of time.

STANDARD & POOR'S 500 *(S&P 500)* – The most widely used external index by fixed indexed annuities. Its objective is to be a benchmark to measure and report overall U.S. stock market performance. It includes a representative sample of 500 common stocks from companies trading on the New York Stock Exchange, American Stock Exchange, and NASDAQ National Market System. The index represents the price or market value of the underlying stocks and does not include the value of reinvested dividends of the underlying stocks.

STOCK MARKET INDEX – A report created from a type of statistical measurement that shows up or down changes in a specific financial market, usually expressed as points and as a percentage, in a number of related markets, or in an economy as a whole (i.e. S&P 500 or New York Stock Exchange).

SURRENDER CHARGE – A charge imposed for withdrawing funds or terminating an annuity contract prematurely. There is no industry standard for surrender charges, that is, each annuity product has its own unique surrender charge schedule. The charge is usually expressed as a percentage of the amount withdrawn prematurely from the contract. The percentage tends to decline over time, ultimately becoming zero.

TRADITIONAL IRA – See <u>IRA (Individual Retirement Account)</u>

TERM END POINT – Crediting methods measuring index movements over a greater timeframe than a year or two. The opposite of an annual reset method. Also referred to as a term point-to-point method. Say that the index value was at 100 on the first day of the period. If the calculated index value was at 150 at the end of the period the positive index movement would be 50 percent (150-100/100). The company would credit a percentage of this movement as excess interest. Index movement is calculated and interest credited at the end of the term and interim movements during the period are ignored.

TERM HIGH POINT *(HIGH WATER MARK)* – A type of term end point structure that uses the highest anniversary index level as the end point. Say that the index value was at 100 on the first day of the period, reached a value of 160 at the end of a contract year during the period, and ended the period at 150. A term high point method would use the 160 value – the highest contract anniversary point reached during the period, as the end point and the gross index gain would be 60 percent (160-100/100). The company would then apply a participation rate to the gain.

TERM YIELD SPREAD – A type of term end point structure which calculates the total index gain for a period, computes the annual compound rate of return deducts a yield spread from the annual rate of return and then recalculates the total index gain for the period based on the net annual rate. Say that an index increased from 100 to 200 by the end of a nine year period. This is the equivalent of an 8 percent compound annual interest rate. If the annuity had a 2 percent term yield spread this would be deducted from the annual interest rate (8 percent-2 percent) and the net rate would be credited to the contract (6 percent) for each of the nine years. Total index gain may also be computed by using the highest anniversary index level as the end point.

VARIABLE ANNUITY – A contract issued by an insurance company offering separate accounts invested in a wide variety of stocks and/or bonds. The investment risk is borne by the annuity owner. Variable annuities are considered securities and require appropriate securities registration.

1035 EXCHANGE – The 1035 exchange refers to the section of tax code that allows annuity owners the flexibility to exchange one annuity for another without incurring any immediate tax liabilities. This action is most often utilized when an annuity holder decides they want to upgrade an annuity to a more favorable one, but they do not want to activate unnecessary tax liabilities that would typically be encountered when surrendering an existing annuity contract.

401(K) ROLLOVER – See IRA Rollover

Made in the USA
San Bernardino, CA
11 September 2015